the
ecology
of
imagination
in
childhood

Edith Cobb

**with an introduction by
Margaret Mead**

Columbia University Press
New York   1977

Library of Congress Cataloging in Publication Data

Cobb, Edith, 1895–1977
The ecology of imagination in childhood.

Bibliography: p.
Includes index.
1. Imagination in children. I. Title.
BF723.I5C6   155.4'13   77-361
ISBN 0-231-03870-4

Columbia University Press
New York and Guildford, Surrey

Copyright © 1977 Columbia University Press
Printed in the United States of America

Acknowledgments

GRATEFUL acknowledgment is made to the Bollingen Foundation, Sally Ellsworth, and the Institute for Intercultural Studies. Grateful thanks are given to all of those who have been involved in the many years during which this book was in preparation, especially Professor Don C. Gifford of Williams College, Edith Cobb's mentor when she began her scholarly writing, and to those who worked on the manuscript and bibliographies, among them Annie Reich, Mary Lausanna Sinclair, Joan Gordan, Ruth Hein, and to Deborah Maine, who completed the arrangement of the manuscript.

This book was written over the course of many years. Therefore some quotations no longer have fully identifiable sources.

Margaret Mead

Contents

the
ecology
of
imagination
in
childhood

Introduction

THE PUBLICATION of Edith Cobb's *The Ecology of Imagination in Childhood* marks the end of a quest that she has shared with me and many others for the past thirty years. This quest originated with the idea that in the imaginative experiences of childhood could be found the essential kernel of the highest forms of human thought. During these thirty years her ideas grew and changed repeatedly. Those of us who followed her quest and shared her ideas incorporated into our own work versions of these ideas, and Edith maintained an eager and animated cooperation with the authors of the books in which she found new insights and fuller statements or illustrations.

This quest was essentially an enterprise with no natural conclusion but was marked by appropriate papers along the way. The first article was published in *Daedalus* in 1959.[1] A paper entitled "Philosophy and the Health of the Child" was presented at a meeting of the American Philosophical Association in 1961, and an article on ecology appearing in a contributed volume in 1909[?] so fascinated certain young ecologists that they were still trying to communicate with her in 1974. In 1961 she received a fellowship from the Bollingen Foundation for a "Study of the Role of Aesthetic Logic in the Natural History of Perception." There followed occasional papers and presentations to learned societies, as Edith Cobb continued to evolve from a highly literate and concerned

1

amateur through varied phases of active professional and scholarly concern.

It was a quest that would never have ended while she was well enough to read another book, watch another child at play in her garden, hear another lecturer present some new piece of research, or read a preprint that one of us had sent her. Therefore, I find the most appropriate way to introduce her book is by a narrative, starting in the summer of 1940, when I first met her, and following through the years when she worked enthusiastically, now with one form of research and now with another, conducting eager correspondences, drafting and redrafting formulations of her developing theory. Many of her most generous collaborators are dead, others have fallen by the wayside, weary of yet another, though better, version of an idea whose earlier forms they had already incorporated into their theoretical approaches. Others who were very young when they started to work with her later became established writers and scholars in their own right and were no longer able to spend the time and energy necessary to wrestle with the astonishing new forms that her adventures took.

I am, indeed, the sole survivor of the whole course of the enterprise and the cooperation that she gave many of us. This cooperation included just the right new book, or a very old one that we needed at the moment, or just the stimulating phrasing that enabled us to take another step. Our mailboxes were stuffed with communications in her elaborate cultivated handwriting, of yet another quotation or another better phrasing of a point. Many of the names that appeared like new stars in her firmament—Peter Goffin, Albert Dalcq, Robert Motherwell, Eduard Lindeman—vanished through the years, their magnificent phrasings replaced by others that she found even more satisfactorily dazzling.[3]

Scientists and poets who once occupied a central position on the stage have been retired to the wings or appear only to recite one line. For example, an early version contained great, relatively indigestible, quotations from the literature on the Rorschach tests; others registered her excitement at the discovery of Evelyn Hutchinson's column in *The American Scientist*[4] and Elizabeth

Sewell's *The Structure of Poetry*.[5] There was a long period when she endured the discipline of social work, yet the reader of the present book would be hard put to explain why her collection of childhood autobiographies was given originally to the Library of the New York School of Social Work in 1958 as part of the Dorothy Hutchinson Memorial Library.[6] Indeed, I don't believe many on the faculty of the New York School of Social Work ever understood what this passionate interpretive explorer of literature and scientific writing had to do with their own professional preoccupations. That collection now has come to rest as a contribution to the Early Childhood Education Library at Teachers College, Columbia University.

Her work spanned the years in which projective tests were elaborated, not yet relegated to the repertoire of the clinical psychologist, the years in which the scientific study of child behavior, embryology, ethology, relationships between biological and poetic form, and new approaches to evolution were themselves developing. Yet it would be impossible to reconstruct the identity of the figures who earlier played a large part in her thesis from this book, which simply ends where she had to stop, because her health no longer permitted her to go on.

I am told by my friends in the field of literary criticism that while the replacement of one insight by another—in more modern dress—is not unusual—nor are books that give no hint of their earlier drafts—the process is seldom documented, and that perhaps my contribution to this enterprise (this "Prelude to a Method," as she calls it) is my knowledge of how it all came about.

In the summer of 1940 an informal conference on the possibility of a documentary film on women's contribution to community life was held in Holderness, New Hampshire at the summer home of Lawrence K. Frank and was convened by Mary Losey.[7] At this conference I met Edith Cobb, who had been an active patroness of social-work institutions and had recently taken an interest in documentary films. We were preparing for the congress celebrating the feminist achievements of Carrie Chapman Catt. Eleanor

Roosevelt's interests had been enlisted, and enthusiasts of every sort were attempting to integrate their interests and realize their hopes within the Congress (as they have been doing, by request, today in the activities of the Bicentennial). It was the heyday of excitement over documentary films; Mary Losey (now Mary Losey Field) had introduced Edith Cobb to the immense capacity of documentary films to give new meaning and insight into social life. It was midsummer; I was trying to finish an early exploration of the newly named science of psychosomatic medicine,[8] nurse my baby, and help two little English girls, sent over from embattled Britain for the duration of the war, adjust to America (which was not yet engaged). The morning of the conference, my nurse–housekeeper, on whom all of our activities rested, threatened to leave and go to work for someone who didn't think she knew so much about how babies should be cared for. All day, my appreciation of the topic of the conference was clouded by uncertainty as to whether Nannie would really leave. As I watched Mrs. Cobb, a woman from a world in which orderly nannies ruled nurseries, we talked about the way in which women's traditional roles could be expanded by opening the walls of the home, giving women more of a role in the community.

Mrs. Cobb, slender and fair with a kind of evanescent, luminous beauty, gently reared and bred, represented the lady about whom Edith Wharton might have written twenty years earlier. A lady with a lady's education only (in Switzerland, England, and a final year at Chapin, graduating in 1914), who had begun, from a suburban base, to participate responsibly on Boards of Directors. (Boards were pretty much of a mystery to me then, entities which I knew about only through my mother's community participation.) Edith spoke with the attenuated tone of voice that can still occasionally be heard from upper-class board members —assured in social position, but frightened and self-deprecating before professionals (who maintained their status by denigrating all unpaid, unprofessional activity). For all of her later years of association with some of the most exciting intellectual groups of our time, Edith never quite lost this mixture of assurance, generously proffered hospitality, shyness, and wonder at being treated as a peer by people who were professional scientists and writers.

Throughout her childhood in a family in which both father and mother enjoyed dramatizing their family life, when few other families took the social rituals of relationships to the outdoors with equal amateur seriousness, she had cultivated an absorbing interest in poetry and autobiography. Similarly, her husband, Boughton Cobb, a businessman who, after the fashion of his architect father, had studied architecture at Harvard,[9] cultivated his deep interest in the natural world. Her interests in literature and her growing concern with psychology and his interest in natural science set them both a little apart from the world they moved in. The sense of their different types of preoccupation also underlay their affiliation with the Democratic Party, in a world where such a political choice was unusual. Their growing interests, the task of rearing their two children, and the coming war, all combined to create an uneasiness, a restless desire for something else.

They moved from the suburbs and the compulsory social life of a beach country club to a New York apartment near Edith's childhood home and a summer place in Falls Village, Connecticut, with a garden presided over by a tiny statue of St. Francis and a house like the playhouses of the imagination, which complemented a child-size playhouse in the garden. Bough had wide meadows and hills where he could band birds and study ferns. Edith's intensive private exploration of books had led her to psychoanalysis. It was a felicitous accident that her analyst was Lillian Malcove, one of the most perceptive child analysts of the day. Thus was set up a dialogue that lasted many years between an analyst who drew her primary insights from the treatment of children and an analysand who was feeling her way toward integrating her lifelong encysted preoccupation with autobiographies of poets, artists, and philosophers with a new theory of the imagination.

That documentary film planned in 1940 was never made, but my friendship with Edith Cobb was established and grew. Edith Cobb's interest in the community of Falls Village was maintained.

She and Bough participated in the activities of the local grange. Later, she kept a diary for me of the small Connecticut town's participation in the war. It became increasingly clear that Edith needed to develop a new kind of identity—one based not on social position but upon a rich social experience and an extraordinary knowledge of poetry and history. She needed to bring her passionate but undirected interests into some kind of focus, to stand on her own among those whom she had formerly entertained or rescued.

As the only professional community of which she had any knowledge was that of social work, she decided to pursue a degree at the New York School of Social Work. I often wondered —I was too busy to find out—what they made of her (she was admitted in 1942, most irregularly I am sure, as a former Board Member) as she dutifully worked her way through to a special certificate in 1948. During her field assignments in medical social work with children, she gained a knowledge of how hospitals functioned and what disciplined insight into human relationships might mean. Her narrative ability was formidable, and she used to tell me in great detail about her child cases and the way she used their play as a guide to possible therapy.

Then in 1948 came the first World Congress on Mental Health in London. Edith was determined to go. It was a congress to which every sort of lay person was admitted, but Edith's inclusion loomed very large in her mind. Through the congress she found Margaret Lowenfeld's Institute for Child Psychology. She introduced me to Margaret Lowenfeld's work on The World Technique,[10] in which child patients worked out their problems by building miniature worlds.

Edith had already begun to formulate, very tentatively, her theory of the significance of childhood imagination. She gave me a one-page formulation in 1947;[11] I showed it to a sophisticated child analyst who sniffed and said, "She's clearly trying to work out her own problems!" But it caught my attention, that of Lawrence Frank, and that of Margaret Lowenfeld in 1949. Her absorption in poetry and the interpretation of poetry, her growing interest in psychology and anthropology, biology and the natural world, fed by her husband's growing expertise, provided her with a number of paths along which she could walk eagerly and rewardingly for those who accompanied her.

In the late 1940s and early 1950s a group of us were engaged in the Columbia University Research in Contemporary Cultures,[12] directed by Ruth Benedict. We used literature and film as material for the analysis of national character. Edith came to know of this, and provided a quondam haven for some of its unusual and gifted participants. Many of them read, with varying degrees of interest, disbelief, and fascination, her manuscript, which by this time had grown to some fifty pages. Geoffrey Gorer commented on the version he saw, that she had made a kind of "prose poem out of the most unpromising materials" as she wove together in startling combinations bits of medical social work, autobiography, and weighty statements by Arnold Gesell and D'Arcy Thompson.

Nicolas Calas was working on his studies of Bosche; Martha Wolfenstein and Nathan Leites[13] were working on their studies of movies; and Erik Erikson came as a consultant on the childhood of Maxim Gorky. Larry Frank was writing, but not publishing, about the way women used their own bodies as a theater and about the importance of literature as a way of understanding human relations. Edith continued to read, to listen, and to feed us with her discoveries of new books and new writers. She seemed at times almost clairvoyant, as she moved around obscure bookshops, selecting books with ambiguous brown spines, which happened to be just what one of us needed at the moment.

She had shifted from the thought of doing any actual social work, to the observation of children's play constructions and spent much time in systematic observation of individual children and children on playgrounds and in schools. She happened into my apartment one day when my daughter had just made a magnificent construction of cardboard, beads, plants, and glass animals, which she photographed and gave me for my records. Robin Bond, who had taught painting at the Summerhill School in England, brought an exhibition of the children's paintings to the

Museum of Modern Art,[14] and the Cobbs became briefly his sponsors. They were deeply impressed with the extraordinary obligations taken on when one sponsored an immigrant and were outraged at the questions that the immigration office asked about Boughton's income. For most of us, who had signed such forms on the basis of practically no financial resources, all of this provided astonishing insights into the ethos of another way of life, deeper understanding of the real contrast between the lives of the intellectual and the privileged, who intermittently enjoyed the products of intellectual creativity.

During the war I planned a dramatization of interprofessional noncommunication for a regional social-work meeting,[15] at which the representatives of public and private agencies, the schools, youth, and board members dramatized their mutual competitiveness, possessiveness, and lack of understanding. I asked Edith to dramatize a typical board member, whereupon she gave a brilliant performance of her sense of the way professionals excluded and denigrated the board members who financed the agencies for which they worked. Then youth, represented by Anatole Holt, now one of our most gifted mathematical linguists, then a senior at the High School of Music and Art, replied with a "pox on all your houses."

The main illumination that I drew from Edith's writing in those days was the idea of a cosmic sense—that human beings need to take in, reshape, and give out, in some altered form, their perception of the natural world, the cosmos. We were all struggling with, first, the definition of basic needs of human beings for food, water, shelter, and sleep, and, second, the more subtle needs for stimulating interaction with other human beings. This came to a head in the studies of maternal separation,[16] of infants who lost the ability to smile when kept without individualized care in even the best orphan asylums. The idea that there was an intrinsic human need for understanding of the natural world, a need as important as the basic needs that human beings share with animals, was an exciting one. The metaphor of "breathing in air," utilizing this air internally and the "breathing" it out in a new form, to be recycled by the natural world, fitted many of our theories about why physically well-cared-for children nevertheless perished, and about the nature of the differences among children reared in stimulating and unstimulating intellectual and artistic environments and different cultures. (Some cultures instigate very few needs and meet them, some instigate deep needs but provide no satisfactory ritual, artistic, or intellectual forms that can fulfill them, and some have become so elaborated that the growing individual is stifled by overdeveloped forms.) So it was in publications in the 1950s that I made my first acknowledgments to Edith Cobb's work.[17]

Edith herself was both living and breathing in the emerging climate of opinion that was to insist on a closer relationship between the humanities and the sciences, enunciate and reject the simplified dichotomy of the *Two Cultures* of C. P. Snow,[18] and bring into the universities living artists and writers instead of critics of dead ones. She insisted on the inclusion of our knowledge of other living creatures in our self-concepts and insisted that there was more to psychological development than the translation of the Oedipal struggle into various forms of sublimation. New discussions of evolution and man's relationship to the natural world and our growing awareness that the natural world was being desecrated and endangered were incorporated in her basic design.

I find the figure of a mosaic the most appropriate image for the work in which she was engaged. The basic design was already evident in the late 1940s, but the choices of pieces for the mosaic —quotations, observations of children, responses to projective techniques, and autobiographical material—were constantly changing. Each version of a chapter contained new pieces that replaced earlier ones. So the work remained fresh and alive—continually renewed as her own imagination expanded with the expanding understandings of the times. This was during the long incubation period of anthropology—between Ruth Benedict's *Patterns of Culture*, Gregory Bateson's *Naven* and his *Steps to an Ecology of Mind*, between Waddington's first essay on science and ethics and *The Ethical Animal*, Caroline Spurgeon's *Shake-*

speare's Imagery and What It Tells Us, Armstrong's *Shakespeare's Imagination*, and Ella Sharpe's *Dream Analysis* and *Our Own Metaphor*, between the *Peckham Experiment* and René Dubos's concept of health.[19] In a sense she could no more finish the book than if she had been an avid child reading her way through a library, constantly renewed with new accessions, suddenly told to stop and call it a day.

But by 1959 the basic design had been filled in enough so that many of us felt it was time to publish at least a statement of her ideas. (Perhaps none of us had yet grasped the way in which the elements in the design of the book would continue to be shifted, replaced, and elaborated.) There was to be a special issue of *Daedalus*[20] in 1959 on current work and controversies to which she, Solomon Barkin, John Bennet, D.W. Bridgman, Réne Dubos, Hudson Hoagland, Seymour Lipset, Lewis Mumford, Howard Simons, Sumner Slichter, and John L. Thomas contributed. Her work was thus quite abruptly catapulted to a new set of appreciative readers to be transformed into a highly personal audience.

As Edith Cobb made her debut in the world of serious *creative criticism*, Boughton Cobb was developing from an enthusiastic amateur naturalist into an authority on ferns.[21] With the evocative interest of Paul Brooks, his *A Field Guide on Ferns* was published by Houghton-Mifflin in 1956. Where Edith's sense of the natural world was mediated by words, Bough's was informed by the banded bird in his hand, the curling tip of a new fern frond. Edith's imagination fed upon the wonder expressed in poems by Keats and Wordsworth, upon the drawings and "worlds" constructed by children. When she seized, with such informed recognition, upon autobiographical material in which Pierre Teilhard de Chardin described his sudden ecstatic feeling for iron, her discoveries grew out of the recorded discoveries of others.

Yet in all of the incorporation of new scientific insights, the changes in a quarter century of excited exploration of the expanding universe, the "Prelude" and the poems of Keats remained central to her thesis. Lawrence K. Frank[22] remained as part of her audience, benefactor, and beneficiary until his death. In some ways they were much alike, never able to complete a work of any length before new winds came to blow the stacked pages aside to make room for yet another new formulation. They were also alike in the way in which other people's most abstract conclusions became raw data for their own creativity. So the *Daedalus* article was published, after agonizing tribulations for the editors (Edith virtually rewrote it in proof, innocently unaware that this was an expensive exercise). But then the discovering and the excited elaboration and expansion of the design began all over again.

The *Daedalus* article closes with a demand for a "redefinition of human individuality," in terms of not only human relations but also man's total relatedness with "outerness," with nature itself. In the 1960s Edith struggled with a new concept—she saw each individual as becoming, in some metaphoric sense, a species in him or herself, the source of new evolutionary changes in human consciousness, creators of essential discontinuities.

In 1971 she had a stroke and from then until the summer of 1973, when Bough died (enormously relieved that Edith's book would at last be published), they both suffered severe physical setbacks. Hence, the final arrangement of the parts of this book has been done by others. But in a sense this was the way she had always worked; she entrusted her manuscripts (while adding inserts to inserts in a progression of elaborations) to a series of editors who devotedly struggled to identify unnecessary repetitions, place quotations, and keep Edith's thinking from being smothered by her enthusiasm for other people's insights. She is very frail now and her sight is almost gone; a granddaughter has designed the jacket of this book. If Edith's strength had not failed, her search would still be continuing; the mosaic would still be changing. There never would have been any good reason to slow or stop the adventure, not even her anticipation of publication. If her strength had lasted five years longer, I can just discern the directions in which her quest would have taken her, for it was this sense of direction in the search, this "prelude to a method" that she gave to all of us.

I had finished *Male and Female*[23] at Cobbweb in Falls Village in 1948, and for many years the village postmistress had to forward letters written to me from odd parts of the globe. Today Cobbweb, with its garden of ferns and the presiding figure of St. Francis, has been sold but the light that emanated from the life that Edith and Bough Cobb lived and the adventures they shared there still suffuses the world of those who knew them.

Margaret Mead

The American Museum of Natural History
New York
September, 1976

NOTES AND REFERENCES

1. Cobb, Edith (1959). "The Ecology of Imagination in Childhood," *Daedalus* Summer: 537–48.
2. Shepherd, P. and McKinly, D. (eds.). *Subversive Science: Essays Toward an Ecology of Man.* Boston: Houghton-Mifflin, 1969.
3. Dalcq, Albert. "Form and Modern Embryology." In L. L. Whyte (ed.), *Aspects of Form.* London: Percy Lund Humphries, 1951, pp. 91–120.
    Goffin, Peter. *Art and Science of Stage Management.* New York: Philosophical Library, 1953.
    Hourd, Marjorie L. *The Education of the Poetic Spirit.* London: William Heinemann, 1949.
    Lindeman, Eduard C. (1940). "Ecology: An Instrument for the Integration of Science and Philosophy," *Ecological Monographs* 10: 367–72.
    Lowenfeld, Margaret. *Play in Childhood.* London: Gollancz, 1935.
4. Hutchinson, George E. *Itinerant Ivory Tower.* New Haven: Yale University Press, 1953.
5. Sewell, Elizabeth. *The Structure of Poetry.* New York: Scribner, 1952.
6. The Dorothy Hutchinson Memorial Library was a part of a special library in the New York School of Social Work, to which Edith Cobb contributed her collection of childhood biographies and autobiographies. When the New York School of Social Work became incorporated into Columbia University, there were objections to the occupation of space by special collections. The Dorothy Hutchinson Memorial Library was then scattered in circulating sections. The Edith Cobb collection was accepted by the Teachers College Library, as breaking it up in the

way that was demanded would have destroyed its usefulness. Dorothy Hutchinson had been Edith Cobb's advisor and supervisor at the New York School of Social Work.

7. The links here are interesting. Mary Losey, as a specialist in documentary films, was working for the American Film Center, financed by the General Education Board, and Lawrence K. Frank had formerly been with the General Education Board. He customarily convened conferences at or near his summer home in New Hampshire. See Mead, Margaret (1969). "Lawrence Kelso Frank 1890–1968," *American Sociologist 4*:57–58.

8. Mead, Margaret (1947). "The Concept of Culture and the Psychosomatic Approach," *Psychiatry 10*:57–76.

9. Henry Ives Cobb (1859–1931) designed the Chicago Opera House, the Newberry Library of the University of Chicago, the Church of the Atonement, the Albany New York Savings Bank, Liberty Tower, and many others.

10. Lowenfeld, Margaret. *The Lowenfeld World Technique.* Memorandum from the Institute of Child Psychology, vol. 6. London: Pembridge Villas, 1954; Lowenfeld, Margaret, manuscript in preparation.

11. Mead, Margaret. "Mental Health in World Perspective." In Marvin K. Opler (ed.) *Culture and Mental Health.* New York: Macmillan, 1959, pp. 501–16.

12. Mead, Margaret and Metraux, Rhoda (eds.). *The Study of Culture at a Distance.* Chicago: University of Chicago Press, 1953.
Mead, Margaret and Wolfenstein, Martha (eds.). *Childhood in Contemporary Cultures.* Chicago: University of Chicago Press, 1955.
Gesell, Arnold. *The Embryology of Behavior.* New York: Harper, 1945.
Thompson, Sir D'Arcy Wentworth. *On Growth and Form.* New York: Macmillan, 1944.

13. Wolfenstein, Martha and Leites, Nathan. *Movies: A Psychological Study.* Patterson, New Jersey: Altheneum, 1970 (first published in 1950).
Nicholas Calas began his studies of Bosche in the early 1950s, and his work is still in progress.

14. Paintings by English adolescents from the Summerhill School, run by A. S. Neill, were shown in the Young People's Gallery of the Museum of Modern Art March 17–April 18, 1948, in an exhibit entitled "Young People's Art Work from an English School."

15. The regional meeting of the American Association of Social Workers was held in New York City in 1943. The panel included Alice Keliher, Anatole Holt, Edith Cobb, and representatives from one public and one private agency.

16. Mead, Margaret. "A Cultural Anthropologist's Approach to Maternal Deprivation." In *Deprivation of Maternal Care: A Reassessment of its*

Effects. Public Health Press Papers, 14. Geneva: World Health Organization, 1962, pp. 45–62.

Bowlby, John. "Mother–Child Separation." In *Mental Health and Infant Development*, 2 vols., Kenneth Soddy (ed.). New York: Basic Books, 1956, I, 117–22.

Tanner, J. M. and Inhelder, B. (eds.). *Discussions on Child Development*, 4 vols. London: Tavistock, 1956–1960.

17. Mead, Margaret (1957). "Toward More Vivid Utopias." *Science* *126*:957–61.

Idem. "Cultural Determinants of Behavior." In *Behavior and Evolution*, Ann Roe and George G. Simpson (eds.). New Haven: Yale University Press, 1958, pp. 480–503.

Idem. *Continuities in Cultural Evolution*. New Haven: Yale University Press, 1964.

18. Snow, C. P. *Two Cultures*. New York: Cambridge University Press, 1959.

19. Benedict, Ruth. *Patterns of Culture*. Boston: Houghton-Mifflin, 1961 (first published in 1934).

Bateson, Gregory. *Naven*. Stanford: Stanford University Press, 1958 (first published in 1936).

Idem. *Steps to an Ecology of Mind*. San Francisco: Chandler, 1972.

Waddington, Conrad H. *The Ethical Animal*. Chicago: University of Chicago Press, 1961.

Idem. *Science and Ethics, an Essay*. London: Allen and Unwin, 1942.

Spurgeon, Caroline F. E. *Shakespeare's Imagery, and What it Tells Us*. New York: Macmillan, 1935.

Armstrong, Edward A. *Shakespeare's Imagination, A Study of the Psychology of Association and Inspiration*. London: Lindsay Drummond, 1946.

Sharpe, Ella. *Dream Analysis; a Practical Handbook for Psycho-Analysts*. London: Hogarth, 1937.

Williamson, George S., and Pearse, I. H. *Biologists in Search of Material: An Interim Report on the Work of the Pioneer Health Centre, Pekham*. London: Faber & Faber, 1938.

Dubos, René. *The Dreams of Reason: Science and Utopias*. New York: Columbia University Press, 1961.

Bateson, Catherine. *Our Own Metaphor*. New York: Knopf, 1972.

20. Holton, Gerald and Strelsky, K. (eds.) (1959). "Current Work and Controversies," *Daedalus* Summer: 383–572.

21. Cobb, Boughton. *A Field Guide on Ferns*. Boston: Houghton-Mifflin, 1956.

22. Mead, "Lawrence Kelso Frank," 1969.

23. Mead, Margaret. *Male and Female*. New York: Morrow, 1949.

ONE

Prelude to a Method

IN THE PRESENT STUDY—the result of over twenty years of research, including extensive fieldwork with children—I am attempting two difficult tasks. The first is to define what is meant by the genius of childhood as a common human possession and a biological condition peculiar to man. The second consists of showing that a major clue to mental and psychosocial, as well as psychophysical, health lies in the spontaneous and innately creative imagination of childhood, both as a form of learning and as a function of the organizing powers of the perceiving nervous system.

Of necessity this exploration of genius requires, on the one hand, relating early psychophysical forces in personal development to those uncommon reaches in human achievement that eventually tend to shape cultural evolution. On the other hand, the time perspectives opened up by an investigation of the biology of creative motivation in childhood ultimately lead to a search for the relationship of child mind to nature. For, unlike all other animal species, the human child displays a spontaneous striving to go beyond biological fulfillment and maturation and to add form and novelty to the environment. The child's urge to "body forth the forms of things unknown" in the microcosm of child art and play bears a distinct resemblance to the morphogenesis characteristic of nature's long-term history, namely, evolution.

By adopting this position when observing the play behavior of the living child and by comparing this behavior with scientific accounts of patterns of morphogenesis and evolutionary history, it occurred to me that child and nature were engaged in some corresponding bioaesthetic striving fundamental to the fulfillment of individual human biological development. The unique patterns of sensory learning and the passionate form-creating striving of each and every child (even within rigid discipline and conformist schooling) resembles evolutionary striving far more than it does growth phenomena, to which genius has already been compared by such investigators and poetic explorers of infancy and childhood as Arnold Gesell.[1] I use the term "poetic" advisedly, in the original Greek sense of *poien*, "to make," a root word that bespeaks the sources of poetic perception in harmonious rhythms of energy systems and those formative processes of the body that are continuities of nature's biological and cosmological behavior.

In order to pursue the theme of the formation of a unique world image by the individual as an integral part of the achieving of a singular identity or self-image, it seemed best, semantically and metaphorically speaking, to translate the older term "psychobiological" into a more explicit and descriptive word, "biocultural." The latter expression indicates more directly the great depths of biological motivation deriving from nature's history that must have contributed to the human impulse to create cultural form and meaning, enabling us to place human individuality in the context of evolutionary history.

In this context the trait that differentiates human nature from animal nature can be more easily observed to consist of man's infinitely greater capacity for individualization. This distinction, I suggest, is such that we must consider each human individual as unique in the expression of his biocultural heritage—almost a biocultural species in himself.

My preliminary research was of necessity literary, for it was sparked by statements by creative adults about their early awareness of some primary relatedness to earth and universe. But, to prove valid, the search for the spirit of childhood as the creative principle in human personality and the source of cultural evolution had to be extended into the most commonplace, severe, and variegated settings of the human struggle for existence. I was not in search of the "gifted" child, the special child, but on the contrary wished to compare the statements of adult geniuses about their childhood recollections with the "natural genius of the child" (in Erik Erikson's phrase).[2]

Beginning with a wide variety of autobiographical recollections, including biographies, letters, diaries, memoirs, and even fiction (in which the role of childhood is nearly always basically autobiographical), I went on to verify my general assumption in work with the living child in everyday life, using formal psychological disciplines, including medical social casework and cultural anthropology.

In order to include both negative and positive polarities in the study of the child's view of the world and methods of integrating world image with body image, fieldwork of necessity included work with the individual child in the family, home, school, hospital, and even in the sadly dramatic setting of children's courts and courts of domestic relations.

The landscapes in which I studied the child's world-building play included playgrounds, both the stony and sterile and the lushly vegetative, the empty or littered city lot or backyards, the country garden and open fields, as well as the beautiful world of sea and sand in which child or man can revel in the wonders of unstructured beauty and movement that release the desire to create in terms of one's particular vision of the nature of things in time and space. Every child, even the handicapped one, must integrate a world image with body image in order to know where and who he is. "Privileged" or "underprivileged," every child tries to structure a world.

If childhood is recognized as the biological phase in each life during which the most actively creative learning takes place, we can understand why this period retains its strength as a biocultural force in cognitive and cultural evolution as well as in personal development.

The need, therefore, is to explore further the role of childhood in personal history and to examine afresh the development of the little human animal learning to transcend his biological nature in order to acquire a cultural heritage. This exploration leads us deep into the history of nature itself and forward into the ecology of imagination in childhood, from which all later creative activities evolve.

It should be clearly understood that throughout I am referring to the child's evolving ability to learn, think, and create meaning in his perceived world, in contrast to the ability to memorize and record other people's interpretations of that world. It is to this genetically motivated process of learning, with intent to acquire creative instruments in order to connect perception and thought, that Wordsworth refers when he speaks of "the world they half create and what perceive" in his poem on personal evolution, *The Prelude*.[3] It is this selfsame capacity to which we refer when we speak of the natural genius, the generating spirit, of the child who must transcend nature psychologically and semantically before he can know the nature he perceives in cultural (i.e., human) terms.

If, as seems apparent, this step is, for each person, a true biocultural transcendence of biological heritage, we must regard individual development not merely as a growth phenomenon, but as a genuine continuation of evolutionary striving. Although this may seem an exaggeration, it is in fact a reinterpretation and enhancement of our knowledge of human nature.

Nature is dynamic and historical. Man is but a fragment of history, but he directs and creates his own history, as well as his *mise-en-scène*, his ecology, for good or ill. Moreover, individual men and women ultimately create cultural and social history in terms of their particular world imagery and their capacity to lead others to participate in the world as they see it, politically, aesthetically, philosophically, or otherwise. We cannot recognize this phenomenon of individuality, which differentiates man from all other animals, unless we accept the idea that at cultural levels each individual is, as it were, a species in himself.

Energy, however, is the "essence" of all behaviors, all motion. All discussions of the nature of energy tend to focus on time and space and on temporal and spatial relations. As this was my focus as I researched the child's morphogenetic impulses and the open-system attitude toward nature, I faced formidable problems prior to the appearance of ecosystems ecology and the definition of ecology as the behavior of energy at differing levels of organization.

Here, at last, the polarities of nature and man began to draw closer together into a relationship that admits the perceptions of the ordinary observer, even at highly abstract levels. In the Whidden Lectures, J. Robert Oppenheimer refers constantly to the simplicities from which great and original abstract ideas often derive. In his lecture "Space and Time," he states his hope that "in some happier future you may feel that mathematics, though a help, is not indispensable for some insight into the essentials of what has been found in modern physics."[4]

However, Oppenheimer emphasizes that no true metaphor (as defined here), mathematical or otherwise, is permanently true, and that this impermanence holds the hope of our cultural future. Using Einstein's and Newton's theories as examples of how great interpretations of physical laws developed from simple perceptual experience, Oppenheimer also refers to the limitations of each theory and concludes that absolute explanations do not exist. Thus, he establishes the nature of two metaphorical fallacies that seem to me to prevent recognition of the lifelong positive role of childhood in personality and, therefore, in general cultural development. The first is the fallacy of permanent norms. The second —allied to it—is the fallacy of permanent maturity that turns up as an implied ideal in medicine, philosophy, and many other modes of thinking. In the long run, these fallacies not only ignore the peculiar value of plasticity of perceptual response to environment in childhood, but also place undue value on seniority, ignoring the inevitable decline of age and the greater rigidity that generally ensues. The second fallacy overlooks the capacity for change in younger men and women, more in tune with the newer velocity of change, especially in this era.

Charles Elton's[5] analysis of the role of the ecologist as a "liaison officer" between apparently unrelated divisions in natural history, organic and inorganic, satisfied my ambition to work with methods already in existence that could be correlated. William Thorpe's[6] relating of evolution, perception, and learning carried me many steps further. But it was not until the July 1964 issue of *BioScience* appeared that my conviction of the existence of a biosynthesis of perception (mind) and cosmos seemed confirmed. Edward Deevey[7] brought the landscape of time into view, and Eugene Odum[8] offered the nonmathematical student schema for the use of ecological function and structure.

Deevey found that "being strongly historical, i.e. in often substituting historical inference for experimental analysis, [ecology] builds firmer bridges toward the humanities and toward the earth sciences as well as toward the social and behavioral sciences than do other kinds of biology." The quotation and the whole article are starred with key terms of the firmament into which research had led me.

Odum's suggestion for recording structure and function as related behaviors seemed to substantiate Oppenheimer's belief that mathematical ideas would find expression in ways open to those who are not mathematically minded:

> Since ecological structure is readily shown in a diagram but difficult to depict in pure mathematics, the electrical analogue circuit diagram or working model has the advantage of simplicity in relating structure and function. The flow chart models are also much easier to understand for most of us who are not skilled in mathematics.[9]

Oppenheimer's and Odum's observations brought to the surface some of my ideas about the use of flowchart models of the child's play behavior originated by Rudolf Modley in *Pictorial Statistics*.[10] This ideographic cross-cultural method of communication, which consists of a reductive simplification of the complex symbolic abstractions of language into symbols in pictorial form, seemed to point toward some valuable clue to a special mode of

communicating with a child. The idea remained dormant, however, until a course in the use of projective techniques, directly
related to work in a hospital setting, brought totally different
reductive methods into relationship with one another.

The gaps between perception and language, the disconnect-
edness of knowledge of all kinds, the enforced discontinuity
between related systems of research and practice, were dramatized for me by this work in a large city hospital in which the
architectural separation of parts of the body and various body
functions into distant wings and even buildings made the person-
in-the-body and the body in its real world very difficult to conceive. Having an eye in wing A, a limb in R, the heart back in B,
and maybe abdominal functioning in X, Y, or Z made the job of
the caseworker, who had at times to cover all of this territory for
the patient as well as the doctor, a phenomenal performance.

Specialization is a necessity in an era such as ours, in which
continual differentiation and proliferation have enriched knowledge to so great an extent. But some centralizing of disciplines,
which would bring into focus the imagery of whole but differentiated human beings as we know them normally—clothed in the
texture, detail, and coloring drawn from their special ecological
niches—seems to be a necessity if we are not to fly apart into
schizophrenic pieces in a breakdown of human relationships as
well as knowledge.

The "crisis" ethos, the continuities and discontinuities of life
within a hospital setting, constantly emphasize the porosity of its
protective walls. Contemporary acceptance of a body–mind continuity has introduced the need to work with the person in the
body–mind combination. In a contemporary hospital, the ethos of
therapy is dominant at both medical and psychological levels,
with biological overtones at medical levels and biological under-
tones drawn from Freudian principles at the level of psychological
work. But the fact remains that although psychological interview-
ing for hospital purposes is still considered to be merely the investigation of personality (the person in the body), the work is
actually an investigation of how the person perceives, takes in,

and integrates this world image with his body image in "real life" outside the temporary world of the hospital.

The need for reduction of experience to primary levels, in order to compress this investigation and to help the person to project or put forth what he cannot say spontaneously, often requires indirect methods—a mapping of the processes of mind. Projective techniques have been invented to fill this gap and to stimulate responses at levels that mediate between language and perception, or questions and answers. That these reductive methods also resemble and derive from forms of play, or play art, fortified my concept of the positive creative aspect of childhood as well as the need for a kind of humility that permits reduction in thought and perception to occur in the adult mind in search of reinterpretation and reorganization of meaning. This idea, which derives from psychoanalysis, points to the need for compassionate intelligence. Creative intelligence also requires the ability to identify and to participate in otherness while retaining a sense of one's own ego–world identity.

It came about, therefore, that by way of the logic of projective methods (including a tree test[11] and a house–tree–person test[12]) that can occasionally be applied to a type of understanding of themes and styles in art, I borrowed from certain studies of art by aestheticians or artists. From *Meaning in the Visual Arts* by Erwin Panofsky[13] I developed a theory of iconography in everyday life. In Paul Klee's *The Thinking Eye*[14] (in which Klee's arguments greatly resemble some of Rorschach's reasoning) I found a cosmogenic description of human gestalt-making endeavor of extraordinary depth and beauty. Love of nature as process and love of knowledge as process are here combined as a unitary action, the mind as body interacting with the universe. Klee's pedagogical lectures are iconographic; he teaches and writes with a pen dipped in love. The diagrammatic illustrations show how spatiotemporal structures in nature and culture are formulated at primordial levels. His narrative explanations allow us to participate in creative acts drawn from all levels of nature's behavior—cosmic, biologic and physiologic—while they remain

essentially simple and formal, even maplike, in design. The cosmogenic nature of the structures of both art and play keep their
links with nature, while transcending it in action and thought.

This capacity to go out and beyond the self derives from the
plasticity of response to environment in childhood, when the
organizing of temporal and spatial relations takes on a deeper
dimension, and where time and space are invitations to greater
creativity and meaning.

The child's ecological sense of continuity with nature is not
what is generally known as mystical. It is, I believe, basically aesthetic and infused with joy in the power to know and to be. These
equal, for the child, a sense of the power to make. Although experience of this "power" is common to all of us, it has as yet hardly
found an articulate place in philosophy, psychology, or biology.
Some efforts to explore the sense of continuity between inner personal state and nonpersonal or nonhuman environment have been
made. But explorations of this type have thus far been heavily
dependent on the language of psychopathology and thus do not
give much help in the search for the sources of the forward
motion of true creativity energized at biological levels. To deal
with these sources, a new vocabulary is surely needed; to be
effective, it must embody a language of technique as well as a diagrammatic vocabulary that can filter down to vernacular use.

Although we have yet to create and apply this vocabulary, it
does seem that we now have the instruments of thought with
which to explore the counterpoint between man and nature and
the ability to pursue our explorations to biophysical levels hitherto
considered totally subjective, hence irrational. In tracing the
sources of this counterpoint, we will, I believe, find ourselves also
following threads of meaning that lead to long-sought unity
between art and science—especially if we begin with the child's
early extrapolation from universals of motion, form, and color.

In the emergent mental climate we are actually well prepared
to think of experience in childhood as the point of intersection
between biology and cosmology, where the structuring of our
world views and our philosophies of human purpose takes place.

We ought, therefore, to be able to cast off the shackles of a super-intellectualism as total technique without abandoning logic at the level of the gestalt. We can then turn our observation of the homespun beauty of the child's thought and play, the child's perceptual worlds, to better use without muddying the waters of adult speculation.

My aim throughout this work was dictated by the belief that a curious combination of negative attitudes toward both the child mind and nature deters us from observing and building upon the innate need and positive desire of every child to create in order to learn and know. Although we speak freely in philosophy—even in the philosophy of the sciences—of the value of the child's sense of wonder to knowledge and learning, without some causal connection, some idea of the sources of wonder in human beings, we know not whereof we speak. Yet the intuitive placing of the child in the midst of the natural world when referring to the sense of wonder is in itself evidence of some biological basis for the attitude of wonder as we have experienced it personally, in "the first poetic spirit of our life."

Unfortunately, the language of conquest still maintains a supreme hold on our social and political theory, our medical policies, and most serious of all, our teaching of ideas about nature and man. Even among naturalists and biologists the realization that in ecology as a biological science we have, for the first time in the history of thought, an instrument for the study of reciprocity and mutuality among categories of thought, as well as among divisions and levels in nature, seems strangely lacking.

Ecology as a science permits us to evaluate reciprocal relations of living organisms with their total environment and with one another as living interdependent systems. This reciprocity includes many "layers" of natural history and extends into a counterpoint between universe and geographical place. Plants, animals, and humans must now be thought of as living in ecosystems, in a web of related, interacting, dynamic energy systems.

If the extrapolations in this work appear to be too sudden or too extreme a use of ecological science, we might say, borrowing

Keats's tender and compassionate line, "Many are poets that do not think it,"[15] that many are ecologists who do not think it and do not recognize it now. Nor are these two statements, one poetic and the other ecological, unrelated, for both have been true of man as a "thinking reed" in search of true metaphor through the millennia. Farmer or fisherman, hunter or natural scientist, poet or explorer, all have had to read nature's behavior ecologically, at different levels of organization and from a poetic viewpoint, in order to achieve a linguistic transformation of perception, an expression of mind's metaphorical relations with nature.

That ecology requires a combination of aesthetic perception and disciplined thinking—a characteristic of true poetry as well —is clearly stated by Charles Elton, who remarked in his work on animal ecology that "there is more ecology in the Old Testament or the plays of Shakespeare than in most of the zoological textbooks ever published!"[16] For the advocates of "purity" of the sciences, an overlapping of the arts and the sciences undoubtedly presents serious psychological hazards. Yet there is increasing evidence in today's biological sciences that subjective and objective levels of mental processes are conjoined in neurophysiology as differing levels of integration.

In a sense, then, my own exploration of the meaning behind what I experienced and sensed was also a journey through both time and space, analyzing and synthesizing, weaving back and forth between the insights of artists and the novel formulations of scientists, between early religious images and the spontaneous activities of today's children. The recognition of the value of true metaphor would seem to be the key to the journey, leading as it does to the ultimate meaning of human transcendence and to the understanding of our most precious tool, compassionate intelligence.

TWO

Wonder as the Genesis of Knowledge

This spiritual elation and response to Nature
is Man's generic mark . . . .
but the true intellectual wonder is first reveal'd
in children and savages and t'is there the footing
of all our temples and of all science and art.
— Robert Bridges, *The Testament of Beauty*

THE SENSE OF WONDER is spontaneous, a prerogative of childhood. When it is maintained as an attitude, or a point of view, in later life, wonder permits a response of the nervous system to the universe that incites the mind to organize novelty of pattern and form out of incoming information. The ability of the adult to look upon the world with wonder is thus a technique and an essential instrument in the work of the poet, the artist, or the creative thinker. The effectiveness of the technique has been emphasized through the ages at the highest levels of intellectual speculation. It was Plato who first defined wonder and designated it as the cause of knowledge, the basis of cognition. In the "Theaetetus," which has for its subject the question, "What is knowledge?" Soc-

27

rates says that the "sense of wonder is the mark of the philosopher. Philosophy indeed has no other origin."[17]

Wonder is, first of all, a response to the novelty of experience
(although not to the totally unexpected, which tends to arouse
anxiety). Wonder is itself a kind of expectancy of fulfillment. The
child's sense of wonder, displayed as surprise and joy, is aroused
as a response to the mystery of some external stimulus that prom-
ises "more to come" or, better still, "more to do"—the power of
perceptual participation in the known and unknown.

When and how do joy and surprise at self and world first make
their appearance? It is certain that through the controlled poise of
his own body, through the sense and vision of his own hands
moving pieces of his world into structure and pattern, the child
first learns to feel the mystery but also the lawfulness of the
cosmos within which he lives. He learns that he may make use of
the lawfulness of nature's materials.

Long before such play structures are possible, however, such
moments as the baby's discovery of his hands and his delight at
their reappearance in his line of vision are marked with a sense of
wonder, an expectancy of more wonders to come; this experience
is also linked to the dim notion that exploration is itself a satisfying process.

In the course of Georg Misch's[18] analysis of the sense of
wonder as expressed in the writings of early cultures in India,
China, and Greece, wonder emerges as a sense of the cosmic.
Wonder is, in fact, the cosmic sense at the stage of questioning in
any language, and primary forms of questioning strongly resemble
the cosmic questionings of the child. The aim of the cosmic questions of both philosopher and child is to obtain, perceptually or
verbally, some reflexive action from the external world to the self,
in order to understand the world in terms of his own experience as
well as through cultural explanations. For the individual, these
are true acts of genesis in the creation of his personal world
image.

Experience in childhood is never formal or abstract. Even the
world of nature is not a "scene," or even a landscape. Nature for

the child is sheer sensory experience, although any child can draw in the wings of his surroundings at will and convert the self into a "theater of perception" in which he is at once producer, dramatist, and star. Therefore, the child's world, his surroundings, are not separated into nature and artifact. His environment consists of the information fed back to his own body by environmental stimuli. This responsiveness includes all levels of the child as a functioning organism. All relations of his body to his surroundings are in this sense natural. In natural science the mutual relations, the adaptive give and take between living organisms and their environment, represent the ecology of the individual organism. In this sense, life is a matter of mutual, functional interaction or intercourse with the environment. This mutuality is equally nourishing and productive of life and form to the mind and to the body.

Human childhood can be generalized as a highly creative, perhaps the most creative, phase in every human life history, a time phase shaped and framed by characteristics shared by all races and all peoples, primitive or sophisticated. Childhood is thus a combination of the uniquely cultural, and therefore human, and the wholly natural, and therefore biological.

Our primary biological peculiarity is our prolonged infancy, our neotenous state, which makes the early, dependent, nidicolous or nestlike nursery condition an intensely important aspect of both personal and biological evolution. The tendency to play and to exploit and expand play, characteristic of this period, can also be said to be characteristic of other animals reared in a nestlike or specifically domestic ecology.

The important distinction, however, is that while other animals do play, the human child's play includes the effort to be something other than what he actually is, to "act out" and to dramatize speculation. Practice play and even "pretense" of a sort are to be found in animal play—as, for example, when dogs pretend to fight yet are prevented by "social inhibition" from serious biting. But a dog never tries to become a horse, a train, a bird, or a tree, while a child may imagine himself to be any one of these organisms or things at will. Unless the child (or the adult) is emotion-

ally ill or schizophrenic and cannot, therefore, establish boundaries to his own body image, the gift of early plasticity in human
nature includes the ability to resume the role of selfhood at will.
This behavior in turn requires a boundaried world within which
to do the acting.

Almost all studies of play seem based on the idea that play is a
matter of games and is primarily a group process. The child's constructive, creative learning, and his cosmopoetic exploration of the
environment, which is only possible within personal and individual
effort, is largely overlooked. I suggest that it is chiefly within the
child's plastic play with blocks, paints, or any amorphous or semi-
structured material (e.g., sand, twigs, and stones), that we can
observe the earliest form of an increasing ability to produce ever
more complex and structured gestalten.

The *dramatis personae* of the child's personal drama are first
and foremost self, mother, and father; his siblings and parent sur-
rogates (in the heavy language of sociology) come next. Biologically and psychologically speaking, parents (known or unknown,
for there must be substitutes) constitute not only the two primary
sources in the child's somatic origin, but also the feminine and
masculine aspects of his psychogenic self, the basic patterns from
which his emotions must develop. However, from birth onward,
human childhood is a process of psychological weaning, from an
instinctual striving toward both parents, by means of exploration
of the environment.

Analysis of purpose in the questions of the child and observation of purpose in both play behavior of children and recollections
of creative thinkers point toward a continuity of attempts at synthesis of self and world, as well as a related motivation toward
learning, that differs markedly from instinct or even insight. Memories of awakening to the existence of some potential, aroused by
early experiences of self and world, are scattered through the literature of scientific and aesthetic invention.

Autobiographies repeatedly refer to the cause of this awakening
as an acute sensory response to the natural world. The motivation
toward creative purpose thus aroused is generally attributed to

intuition, a flash of recognition. Thus, although the question of intuition has been analyzed through the ages, I choose to consider it here not as a mystical or specialized type of vision, but quite simply as an aspect of perceptual learning, one resembling "latent learning" in animals but possessing the potential for creating novelty of meaning.

Walt Whitman soared to fame on the wings of his recall of perception in childhood. His description of cognitive processes in his own childhood comes near to being a definition of method. His poem on the child's learning through identification is a classic example of what Giambattista Vico[19] refers to as the "vulgar wisdom" of child and poet. The poem is a singularly apt explanation of the dynamics of the ecology of the child's imagination, that perceptual interplay between self and world which, in my own researches, I observed as a generality in the world play of the child. Whitman exclaims of himself:

> There was a child went forth every day,
> And the first object he looked upon, that object he became,
> And that object became part of him for the day or a certain part
>   of the day,
> Or for many years or stretching cycles of years.
> The early lilacs became part of this child,
> And grass and white and red morning glories, and white and red
>   clover, and the song of the phoebe-bird,
> And the Third-month lambs and the sow's pink-faint litter, and
>   the mare's foal and the cow's calf.[20]

However, not only the softer textures of spring appealed to the child, but also "the noisy brood of the barnyard" and "the mire by the roadside." Childhood's willing acceptance and enjoyment of the muck and mire of life completes this power of creating mutual relations with the total environment and further empowers understanding at all levels of controlled thought in later life.

For the young child, the eternal questioning of the nature of the real is largely a wordless dialectic between self and world. When language renders this confrontation articulate, it becomes an undertone to all persistent questioning by the child. The adult who senses this need and responds with integrity to the child's inquiries will find the child's heart and mind linked with his own.

Whitman poignantly recalls the search for

> The sense of what is real, the thought, if after all it should prove unreal,
> The doubts of day-time and the doubts of nighttime, the curious whether and how,
> Whether that which appears so is so, or is it all flashes and specks?
> Men and women crowding fast in the streets, if they are not flashes and specks, what are they? (Ibid.)

It is no mean task to keep a balance in dealing with this questioning of reality, for within the orbit of the child's experience the value of fantasy and imagination is of the deepest importance; yet fear of fantasy runs very high. The balance, however, is most deeply dependent on earthly roots in sensory experience. At the level of participation in nature during childhood, there is fusion between emotion as the energy of spirit and the spirit of place as the energy of the behaving world.

Bernard Berenson writes in his autobiography:

> As I look back on fully seventy years of awareness and recall the moments of greatest happiness, they were for the most part, moments when I lost myself all but completely in some instant of perfect harmony. In consciousness this was due not to me but to the not-me, of which I was scarcely more than the subject in the grammatical sense. . . . In childhood and boyhood this ecstasy overtook me when I was happy out of doors. Was I five or six? Certainly not seven. It was a morning in early summer. A silver haze shimmered and trembled over the lime trees. The air was laden with their fragrance. The temperature was like a caress. I remember—I need not recall—that I climbed up a tree stump and felt suddenly immersed in Itness. I did not call it by that name. I had no need for words. It and I were one.[21]

The joy expressed here is the joy of recognition, a delighted awareness that knowing and being are in some way coincident and continuous within a larger process and that this kind of know-ing is in itself an achievement of psychological balance.

Berenson pays tribute to the child's early realization of some profound value in experiencing the nonpersonal order of nature. The imagery is confined to the level of sheer behavior, of being a consciously behaving self in a behaving world, a world in which body and universe are engaged in some harmoniously integrated ongoing process.

This participation in experience is a direct organic participation of the perceiving nervous system in systems of nature, a sheer unbounded psychophysical experience of nature as cosmos, evok-ing a passionate response which, despite Freudian interpretations of the origins of passion, is not erotic. The exaltation that the child feels is a passionate response to an awareness of his own psychophysical growth potential as a continuity of nature's behavior. This pattern of response is intimately connected with the needs of mental (i.e., spiritual) health.

There is no romantic nostalgia in Berenson's recollection, no self-adulation in this recollection by a gifted man. "Surely most children are like that," he remarks, but continues, "I have retained that faculty through the years and can still melt into a good story, into its character, its events, its tempo to such a degree that my diaphragm loses its flexibility."[22] Meanwhile, as a result of this sense of continuity of personal experience, the early pattern of thought is established, and subsequently it becomes a method or technique.

Berenson notes that in later life he has "never enjoyed to the utmost a work of art of any kind, whether verbal, musical, or visual, never enjoyed a landscape, without sinking my identity into that work of art, without becoming it,"[23] although he always remains "the wee homunculus" of a perceiving subject.

I have chosen passages from Berenson, not from any preference for his aesthetic views, but because he gives an exceptionally full and clear analysis of the relationship between the child's way of "knowing by becoming" both plastically and dramatically—that is to say, both on the level of perceptual participation and the more commonly understood level of identification with living figures and forms in the external world.

Continuing his discussion of childhood experience in relation to his later knowledge, Berenson speaks of himself as "an energy of a given force of radiation and of a certain power of resistance," but he adds that at the age of seventy he seems to "be the same in these respects that I remember being when I completed my sixth year."[24] This was when he first sensed consciously, although preverbally, the harmony of his body and the harmony of nature—the power of standing, moving, playing, modeling, or just being in the world around him as a part of a universal aesthetic logic in nature's formative processes. A child reads the imagery of experience and often perceives preverbally the logic of relationships that are overlooked in later, more formally fixed and intellectualized systems of knowledge.

Barfield argues that "men do not *invent* those mysterious relations between separate external objects, and between objects or feelings or ideas. . . . These relations exist independently, not indeed of Thought, but of any individual thinker."[25] He quotes Bacon's "Advancement of Learning": "Neither are these only similitudes, as men of narrow observation may conceive them to be, but the same footsteps of nature, treading or printing upon several subjects or matters." Bacon also believed that Nature must be read as the Book of Creation from the level of a child's view. "Treading" and "printing" express the immediacy of preverbal sense experience and perception.

It is to these intuitively perceived relationships that I refer when I speak of true metaphors. "The language of primitive men," Barfield adds somewhat later, "reports them as direct perceptual experience. The speaker has observed a unity, and is not therefore conscious of *relation*." At this level language expresses a latent awareness of "the principle of living unity" (ibid.), which is assuredly a latent awareness of ecological relatedness.

True metaphor seems to derive from the overlapping of the energies of the perceiving nervous system and energy systems in nature at the level of unity which is the specific interest of ecol-

ogy, where temporal and spatial relations are of supreme importance in the drive toward organization of form and meaning.

Sir Herbert Read, discussing the newer scientific understanding
of the basis of perception, finds that perception is not only a pat-
tern-making, pattern-selecting function of gestalt formation, but
also an activity actually made possible by the fact "that pattern is
inherent in the physical structure or in the functioning of the
nervous system." Therefore, it follows "that matter itself analyzes
into coherent patterns or arrangements of molecules" and "that all
these patterns are effective and ontologically significant by virtue
of an organisation of their parts which can only be characterised
as *aesthetic.*"[26]

This is certainly equivalent to saying that within the behavior
of the nervous system we find the primordial level of the form-
creating behavior that produces the forms we recognize as aesthetic in art. Art, however, becomes art only through a further
organization of nature's materials that transcends the meaning of
nature itself. In transcending the meaning of nature, the iconography of the arts can change the meaning and raise the value of
our perceptual relations with nature and the world, nonverbally
as well as verbally. Although the creativity of child and adult are
by no means the same, we own our power to reduce meaning in
order to reconstruct it to our prolonged human infancy and childhood. The ability to maintain plasticity of perception and thought
is the gift of childhood to human personality; this truth is sorely
abused, in our attitudes not only toward the child in society, but
also toward the child in ourselves.

To quote Paul Klee again:

> There must, after all, be some common ground between laymen
> and artists, where they can meet halfway and the artist will no
> longer look like a mere eccentric, but like a creature set down
> unasked, as you were, in a world of innumerable forms, and who,
> like you, must get his bearings in it as best he can. Who differs
> from you only in that he manages by his own specific means and
> methods, and that sometimes, perhaps, he is happier than the
> uncreative man, who cannot achieve release through art.

You will surely grant the artist this relative advantage, for he has it hard enough in other respects.

Let me use a parable. The parable of the tree. The artist has busied himself with this world of many forms and, let us assume, he has in some measure got his bearings in it; quietly, all by himself. He is so clearly oriented that he orders the flux of phenomena and experiences. I shall liken this orientation, in the things of nature and of life, this complicated order, to the roots of the tree.

From the roots the sap rises up into the artist, flows through him and his eyes. He is the trunk of the tree.

Seized and moved by the force of the current, he directs his vision into his work. Visible on all sides, the crown of the tree unfolds in space and time. And so with the work.

No one will expect a tree to form its crown in exactly the same way as its roots. We all know that what goes on above cannot be an exact mirror image of what goes on below. It is clear that different functions operating in different elements will lead to sharp divergencies.

And yet some people would like to deny the artist the very deviations that his art demands. They have even gone so far in their zeal as to accuse him of incompetence and deliberate distortion.

And yet all he does in his appointed place in the tree trunk is to gather what rises from the depths and pass it on. He neither serves nor commands, but only acts as a go-between. His position is humble. He himself is not the beauty of the crown; it has merely passed through him.[27]

Here the tree is image, symbol, and metaphor, a true representation of mind in evolution.

THREE

Anatomy of the Sense of Wonder

THE HUMAN MIND is of necessity individual, unique, and dependent on boundaries; the contemporary picture of nature as known to art and science, on the other hand, is cosmic and dynamic and continuous. Human identity depends, therefore, on a sense of both discontinuity and continuity with nature as history. Testing of the self against the bounded and the unbounded begins within the spatiotemporal relations of mother and child and continues into play and the iconography of play art.

The notion that the child lives in a timeless world seems an adult projection upon the child of totally adult wishes and fantasies—including perhaps an adult wish to return to prenatal peace. I would say that the child is deeply aware of himself as an unfolding growth phenomenon, a living bit of spatiotemporal extension. His entire body is a figure of "the principle of expectancy," temporal sequence and spatially changing form. The small child is, in fact, consistently, even when nonverbally, concerned about when and where events will happen, even before he is able to think in terms of how or why.

An example drawn from Freud[28] demonstrates the urge to organize spatiotemporal relations latent in the manifest dramatic interest and behavior of the child. An eighteen-month-old boy, playing in his crib with a spool and a length of string, comforts

37

himself during his mother's temporary absences from the room by throwing the spool out onto the floor and drawing it back again, murmuring, "Mama, Mama." Mothers go, but they do come back again—this is the message the spool gives the child, in Freud's view. Nevertheless, at eighteen months a spool is a "thing" and a mother is a mother, and the fascination of testing time and space is a most common pattern in play behavior, although its importance at this age is generally overlooked.

The child in this example is experimenting with the behavior of the nonhuman environment quite as definitely as with the problem of his mother's absence. Mothers and spools extend beyond the body, but strings tied to "things" enable a child to limit a temporal sequence and temporal extension. Such an explanation does not undermine or detract from Freud's interpretation. It merely adds depth to life's dramatic themes while pointing to a use of the body's energies more closely related to individual human survival. The need to extend the self in time and space—the need to create in order to live, to breathe, and to be—precedes, indeed, of necessity exceeds, the need for self-reproduction as a personal survival function.

Grammar and syntax are modes of working linguistically with temporal and spatial relations, uniting sight (in the written word and verbal image) and sound (of spoken language) and inner awareness and outer form in culturally organized relationships. The little child first acts out a preverbal method of knowing with his body and with the first layers or levels of mind. This acting out tends toward rhythmical pattern and continuity, enjoyment of sing-song sounds. Only later can exploratory patterns be given thematic sequence.

We can say that for the child, time as a process has no discernible boundaries but does have temporal sequence from a sensory point of view. This preintellectual sense of boundlessness is thus unbounded temporal sequence as well as spatial plasticity. (Will the blocks go higher? When will the sandcastle fall?) The universe into which the past processes of evolution have poured the manifold richness of natural forms, the universe from which the ordering forces that create the body derive, is the selfsame universe to which the child spontaneously attempts to add new forms in play.

The child's posture and behavior are addressed to the future; his expectations and hope are greater than at any other period in life history except when intuition and expectancy are aroused and mobilized in later life by the need to project the imagination. That a "spiritual elation and response to nature is Man's generic mark" is evident even in early childhood if it is recognized that the child's delight in the power to model and mold with hand and eye and mind is aroused by a physical and physiological awareness of his own ability to organize temporal and spatial relations and create a world within which to find his own identity, beginning in the beautiful, comparative, metaphorical work of preverbal form-creating play behavior. At this stage of the life cycle the whole organism speaks to nascent "spirit in ditties of no tone," to use Keats's phrase.

"Elation" as the child's generic response to the surrounding world is first of all physical. The awakening of intellectual wonder, which is the response of the human nervous system to the external world, begins in the earliest coupling of the tiny organism with its environment, as the infant eats or breathes. In infancy, the sense of futurity awakened throughout the touch systems of the child's body are memorable excitations that may later "send, through all this fleshly dresse, bright shootes of everlastingnesse."[29]

The anatomy of the sense of wonder, which Plato recognized as the source of cognitive development and theoretical knowledge, must therefore be sought, it seems, in the physiology of nervous systems and the evolution of perception in animal species. This approach to evolution is already highly developed in the science of ethology, the comparative study of animal behavior. William Thorpe[30] equates perception and learning with animal evolution from the single-celled creature on up to the highest multicellular organism.

In sum and substance, Thorpe's position—which gives the most support to the concept of the relationship between human perception, intuition, imagination, and learning presented in this work —may be *mapped* in brief as follows: with the appearance of animal organisms there also appears what we define as perception. According to Thorpe, an animal of even the most primitive protozoan type may be defined as "something that perceives." In his extended historical description of the unfolding of an increasing differentiation and complexity of behavior in living things, he states that *"perception is a first-order drive."* With the emergence of nervous systems, the need to organize the environment becomes one of the most fundamental of all perceptual activities.

In discussing the evolution of nervous systems, Thorpe maintains that these functional systems must have evolved because some "primitive conative faculty of insight inherent in the very nature of perception must have been part of the very early stages in the development of living organisms." The logic of this phase of Thorpe's argument leads to the concept that "motivation for learning is central and neural and that organized and proliferated cognitive structure itself is the goal toward which learning moves."[31] Learning in this sense (as overtly stated by Thorpe) serves as its own reward. Thorpe notes:

> It is concluded that there is now substantial and precise evidence for a general drive in a number of animals, and that this can be looked upon as an indication of primary motivation which to some extent, however slight, is superior to the governing centres of any of the instincts or of their combinations, and finds its most characteristic expression in exploratory behavior in all its various forms. It is closely linked with ideas of "expectancy" and "purpose."[32]

This concept is already implied in general developmental theories in which synthesis and integration are fully recognized and exploited as fundamental dynamic—or better, behavioral—patterns of life. "Motility," writes Charles Herrick, "is the cradle of mind."[33] Gesell traces the experiential sequence of the growth behavior of the body toward mind as a biological phenomenon, from the fetal stage on up to its elaboration into the expressions of genius of adulthood. "The embryogenesis of mind," he notes, "must therefore be sought in the beginnings of postural behavior" in prenatal beginnings.[34]

"The fetus," Gesell tells us, "is a growing action system. . . . Its first and foremost function is to adjust to the ceaseless pull of gravity."[35] This experience permeates all later behavior and is the primary adaptation to the logic of nature's aesthetic, formative lawfulness. Eventually "postural attitude issues into postural action" as these early layers of information extend into behavioral forms and patterns.

It is perhaps self-evident that in any choice of position or attitude toward the outer world, the entire body—its tonus and tension, its neuromuscular, sensorimotor apparatus—are involved in perceptual effort and achievement. In addition, all purposeful creativity must of necessity be based on a sense of forward movement, a "feed-forward," an expectancy of reaching a goal, however dimly realized. For the child or the poet in every age and culture, the prelude to metaphorical ways of knowing the world begins in this primordial perceptual activity.

An unusually apt illustration of these points is found in Vladimir Nabokov's *Speak, Memory: An Autobiography Revisted*, which he closes with descriptions of his own little boy's experiences and behavior, observed and described in mid-twentieth-century cosmic terms. After describing the tiny child's responsiveness to varied types of locomotion (the result of technological improvement in prams and toys), he recounts the effects of these on the baby's evolution. The boy progressed from the well-rubbered, deep-springed, lace-curtained vehicle of infancy to a lighter make, in which the baby managed to stand up, "less like the groggy passenger of a pleasure boat than like an entranced scientist in a spaceship," to a stroller in which the little boy began to manage motion, until finally, at the age of two," he received a four-foot-long, silver-painted Mercedes." At this point "a new wave of evolution started to swell, gradually lifting him again from the ground,"[36] which the stroller had helped him to reach on foot.

"Besides dreams of velocity, or in connection with them, there is in every child the essentially human urge to reshape the earth, to act upon a friable environment."[37] Changes in the meaning of motion, Butterfield maintains, are basic to the rise in levels of thought.[38] Nabokov continues:

> Rapid growth, quantum-quick thought, the roller-coaster of the circulatory system—all forms of vitality are forms of velocity, and no wonder a growing child desires to out-Nature Nature by filling a minimum stretch of time with a maximum of spatial enjoyment.[39]

When, in addition to this insight, Nabokov adds that "innermost in man is the spiritual pleasure derivable from the possibilities of outtugging and outrunning gravity, of overcoming or re-enacting the earth's pull" (ibid.), we can link this intuition directly to Gesell's analysis of the embryogenesis of mind in the prenatal functional adaptation to the ceaseless pull of gravity.

The experience of motion and problems of motion are part of the deepest experiences known to man. But such problems also constitute the motivating force in man's passionate and successful endeavor to animate the inanimate. This desire is not only the basis of all human technical invention, it is also a prime characteristic in the creation of effective metaphor. According to Aristotle, "Those words set a thing before the eyes which show it in an active state."

We can relate this statement from ancient Greece to a discovery of modern psychology, Rorschach's inkblot test, in which the human power of perceiving figures in terms of motion is seen as a law of perceptual and psychological behavior. The test—or, as Rorschach defines it, the experiment—likewise discloses that motion in thought has quantitative limits. The mind must work toward the organization and creation of form if it is to avoid a dangerous fluidity.

According to the rationale of this experimental analysis of perception, logical thinking—aesthetic or scientific—must relate inner process to outer reality. From this it may be judged that perceptual behavior is a composite of levels of bodily behavior, an expression of matter as patterned energy, the wholeness of this hierarchical continuum achieving ultimate expression through "the integrative action of the nervous-system."[40]

For the child, time and growth are organically and perceptually equated, for growth is a sensed experience of movement in time. Rhythm for the child is experienced in the dancing blood, the dancing heart, the beating pulse; rhythm, like motion, is a cosmic experience, in fact, and the child's "world making" is a continued cosmic speculation in the form of a recreation and rearrangement of parts of the environment into synoptic wholes in which the self exists.

The body continues its history as a unitary action system postnatally, gradually accumulating "homeostatic wisdom," and assimilating actions and patterns as the dynamic substrate of all cognition and thinking. This physiological "wisdom shows itself not only in the single moment but in the stretching cycle of the life career."[41] Life itself is acted out historically in the behavioral patterns of regulation and integration, among which "respiration remains the most crucial of all behaviors for integrative as well as for regulatory purposes" (ibid.). If the counterpoint with gravity is fundamental to the effort to know and to be, respiratory reactions form the substrate of the expressive behavior of speech. While "in subvocal speech, the ghosts of patterned respirations become the attenuated vehicles of phantasy and thought" (ibid.).

Respiration plays a major role in creative mentation as well as in the health of mind, for respiration is essential to the illumination of consciousness that energizes the soul and maintains evolutionary striving. In depression, a depreciation in respiratory reactions is a major symptom, while respiration as experience comes closest to providing the mind with a vivid counterpoint between life and death.

The highest centers of cerebral activity, also the most recent in evolution, have the greatest metabolic need. Therefore, as Gesell notes, maintaining his poetic–scientific tone, "The highest acts of integration are to this extent dependent upon exquisite perfection in the menial acts of respiration" (ibid.).

For this and many other reasons we cannot by-pass the humble vulgarities and menial acts of the body in infancy and childhood, or even in adult life, in our efforts to elevate thought processes. When we attempt to do so philosophically, we not only skip the all-important woman–child relationship, but also lose awareness of the physical counterpoint between the microcosm of the body and the macrocosm of the universe. In so doing, we disconnect our salient human characteristic, our intuitive cosmic sense, from its purposeful base in technological health, to paraphrase Michael Polanyi, who defines physiology as "the technology of healthy achievements."[42]

Physiology is purposeful in the sense that organs have evolved for definite purposes, Polanyi argues, and in the use of these organs "man the innovator and explorer" is seen as a creature "passionately pouring himself into an existence closer to reality" (ibid.). If man is evolution become conscious, surely this is due to his own consciousness striving to join forces with the universe in this passionate pursuit of the realities of temporal and spatial relations. For each individual, however, the drive toward exploration has its beginnings in the instrument of the developing nervous system.

According to Gesell, there is only one embryology of behavior, which begins to unfold before the infant is born. Whereas Gesell defines genius as a continuity of this beginning and calls it a growth phenomenon, I would define genius as *an evolutionary phenomenon, at biocultural levels, beginning with the natural genius of childhood and the "spirit of place."*

FOUR

The Ecology of Perceptual Organization

THE OPEN-SYSTEM attitude toward unparticularized sensory experience is characteristic of childhood. It evokes what I have suggested can be defined as cosmic sense, a sense of futurity and "onsight," which links ecologically with insight, creating a sense of the power to organize time and space, imagine form, and achieve a future in knowledge.

The energies of nature impinging upon the nervous system meet in the open-system, questioning attitude of child or man. The search for perceptual form and meaning in the perceptually unknown evokes a conjugation of mind and nature. At this level animate and inanimate are unified in the living systems of the behaving organism.

Some awareness of a potential futurity must be awakened in the earliest postnatal intake of breath, in the metabolic "appetite" of brain cells, as Gesell's studies of neonatal infancy suggest. Later the elation, termed "spiritual" in this work—the expression of energy as formative impulse awakened in the nurturing arms—becomes the source of the "poetic" creative principle from which the mind of child or poet derives.

It is especially interesting to note, therefore, that in dictionary terms the word "animate" derives from a Latin word signifying soul or breath (a metabolic action pattern), and that among its meanings are "to give spirit to" or "to put in motion or operation" or, synonymously, "to energize." The term "genius" plays with all these threads of meaning, including mental power or energy, but in its earlier usage it referred most frequently to the spirit of place, the *genius loci*, which we can now interpret to mean a living ecological relationship between an observer and an environment, a person and a place.

Basically, the process of creativity reduces itself to mapping and traveling, picture and explanation, gestalt-making process and thematic apperception that is a serial linking of gestalten in time. Key terms tend to mobilize thought processes into constellations or psychological landscapes, in which the journeying, exploratory mind can continue to find its way toward definitions of reality as distinct from fantasy. "Mapping" is one such key term.

The journeying mind in search of reality is analytic but moves toward synthesis. Its purpose is diagrammatical and creative; it employs a map-making process of identifying and charting a terrain that must be held in memory for future reference. However, just such a descriptive explanation holds also for simple acts of perception as in childhood. According to Elsasser,

> The process of mapping an optical image of the external world upon the retina, whence it is again mapped in a different but precise fashion upon the cerebral cortex, whence it is operated upon by pattern-recognition devices: all this requires apparatus of an extraordinary degree of precision. The same applies of course to the sound-analyzing devices of the ear and to their cerebral correlates. No amount of argumentation about feed-back-endowed, self-stabilizing mechanisms can detract from the fact that the underlying indispensable information content is extremely large. By far the most complex organ in a human being is the nervous-system and the brain.[43]

"Map" and "mapping" are thus both *key terms*. They express an immediacy of experience of organism and environment that has been extended, extrapolated, and transformed into speech as well as into systems of behavior, specifically, map-making and map-using. In other words, the verbal image of a map or mapping mobilizes and fuses the spatiotemporal experience of the perceiving nervous system into a form that has in turn become a symbolic abstraction, a condensation of level upon level of experience and information fused into symbol and code.

Thomas Pollock notes that "the making of a theory is like the making of a map. It does not discover new territory; it analyzes certain existing relationships."[44] Mapping follows exploration, which awakens or arrests the relational map-making type of attention and permits condensation into symbolic pattern or form.

Yet if insight develops through learning as an innate instinctual process in animal life, we have to ask ourselves at what point man developed the momentous depth of speculation about time and space that underlies human inventiveness. This seems to be the point at which the greatest differences between the perceptions and learning ability of humans and other animals occur. Perception, whether animal or human, is a building of primary perception of relations and parts into more and more complex and unitary systems. Even on human levels, where perception becomes a part of thought systems within the framework of speech, these processes are maintained by the perceptual connection of those inner and outer worlds between which we travel all our waking lives. These perceptions are maintained on many levels, but because of our complex eyes, vision has undoubtedly been the ruling experience in the development of human culture and language. Intuition, therefore, can be considered to be a type of "seeing," stimulating in turn the organizing process we call imagination.

All animal perception can be said to remain instinctual—to remain perceptual information, in fact—even when insight and comparison with memory are active. In contrast, human perceptual processes can be said to have been transferred into systems of language and thought above and beyond the images perceived; the child begins by having to match what is seen with what cannot be seen—the experience of other people who have created his language and culture.

The child therefore becomes a taxonomist, for human learning requires a constant process of classification of both experience and things. The scientifically or philosophically inventive mind as well as the mind of the poet must retain this capacity in later life if its creative purposes are to be actively maintained or fulfilled. Indeed, taxonomy—in the purely scientific sense in which Michael Polanyi uses it—is essentially similar to artistic endeavor, highly personal and aesthetic in its working.

Generative gestalt formation (the ability to perceive, classify, and name new patterns in relations) is the working of intuition, which we find at the source of all original thinking. This type of creative purpose is clearly present in the child's formative efforts in play. Play can be observed to be a sort of "fingering over" of the environment in sensory terms, a questioning of the power of materials as a preliminary to the creation of higher organization of meaning.

In assuming such an attitude toward development of the body and the mind, we open the way to the further observation that the primordial perceptual experience that remains a living drive and permeates all the organs and cells of the body, is the dynamic experience of self and world as a temporal and spatial continuum.

For every child all the world is new, and freshness of sensory experience abounds. While for animals meaning remains functional and perceptually based, for the human child perceptual adaptations must be semantically correlated with the pattern and customs of his culture and era. But meaning in the world of child or man requires something more profoundly related to nature than can be rendered by the visual or verbal image alone. To be meaningful, the dimension of time must achieve expression in some pattern. Like music and other coordinations with biological rhythm that transcend sheer animal heritage, language must achieve sequence, must have beginnings and endings, and must possess some characteristics of the "good gestalt" that give shape and structure to meaning, whether in the linear causal sequences emphasized in Western cultures or in the reticulate approach to knowledge and perceptual worlds more characteristic of many Eastern and preliterate cultures. The reticulate image of nature and knowledge clearly derives from intuitive levels that are closer to sensory experience and the earth, even when they are elaborated to high levels of sophistication in technology as well as in art, as is the case with the ancient Chinese. The linear, more time-conscious cultural world imageries of Western civilizations have evolved as intellectual structures ultimately dominated by the sciences.

Neither of these approaches to knowledge, however, can function effectively without the presence of the other. Intuition remains "guesswork" until interpreted and given shape by intellect; intellect, unless it is serviced by sensory experience and intuitive levels, becomes mechanized, computerized memory—colorless and dehumanized.

Intuitive sensibility and intellectual intent are present at any level of discourse. Whether in the vernacular of everyday speech or in the rhythm and balance of poetry, in the charming sounds of the infant's babble or in the formal declamations of playwrights or statesmen, the need to organize sound and sense into some kind of sequence and to include *motion* in the structuring of time and space appears to be instinctual in human beings. That animal "voices"—of bird or beast, fish or insect—display a similar need to pattern sound suggests that an evolutionary process has come to a climax in human speech and general aesthetic expression. This climax embodies the very evolutionary potential and continuity that brought these forms of expression into being.

To repeat Thorpe's great point, perception is an "active organizing process, itself possibly including an element of purpose."[45] Therefore, he writes, "perception is obviously a process in time rather than an instantaneous event," and later continues, "It seems safe to say that perception of a time dimension including an element of expectancy is as fundamental to organisms as is perception of space."[46]

In early childhood an elaboration of what Thorpe defines as the "principle of expectancy," inherent in the nervous system of higher animals, is clearly in evidence. Expectancy leads to an appetite for exploration for which getting to know the environment is its own reward. The significant point of resemblance between the animal's and the child's explorations of environment is that in either case expectancy must involve the dimension of time as neural experience and an aspect of the behavioral route toward the act of gestalt-making in space. What differentiates the human from the animal exploratory behavior is the human need to express temporal experience by giving it continuity and sequence in *narrative* (i.e., story form). Even a tiny baby "talks" to himself sequentially before experience has semantic meaning. So a student of Shakespeare's world imagery may say that Shakespeare led a life of allegory; his works are the comment on it. But our individual lives are of enormous "worth" to each and every one of us, and every man's life is a continual autobiography, even in early childhood.

A moment's reflection will bring to mind the amount of time spent imagining, composing, or restructuring scenes of daily life. In order to "make sense" of our lives, we are obliged to give them a spatiotemporal setting and narrative form. The highest poetic endeavor has its inception in the child's need to be what he wants to understand, and to express that knowledge in some outward form. Thus the life history of a child is an ascension out of biological history into the world imagery of his particular culture and the language of his particular era.

According to Michael Polanyi, a theory of the universe is implied in language itself, because by being prepared to speak in our language on future occasions, we expect it to apply to the future of our experience. "These expectations form a theory of the universe, which we keep testing continuously as we go on talking about things."[47] This is certainly the equivalent of saying that language is cosmological by nature and in intention and that it is the specific mode of behavior by means of which man knows and feels he is managing time and space. Once this concept is absorbed, it is quite easy to see that the child's early desire to master language is part of a basic human need to move forward from unstructured form into a theory of the universe, to create meaning, and so to discover himself in time and space.

We must therefore consider the wish to narrate, to make a "story" in order to "know" both continuity and discontinuity, arrest and movement in spatiotemporal structure and pattern, as an instinctual human urge, first expressed in the form of myth, and even earlier in song. An instinct toward narration and the creation of narrative form is probably innate in man as the only "time binding" animal.

Alfred Korzybski's concept of time binding is essentially an idea of language structure and intellectual processes at semantic levels.[48] The addition of a time dimension at the level of all gestalt perception gives us access to ideas of temporal experience as a part of all recognition. It actually "takes time" to make an image with the eye, although the velocity of gestalt perception prevents any fully conscious awareness of this organic behavior. Nevertheless, in dance, song, story, or the formal story that we refer to as history, we act out our fundamental awareness of time and our need to shape it. Time binding in semantic form permits each generation to advance from the point at which the preceding one left off, making it possible for genius to produce cultural mutations in a single leap, as with Einstein's theory of relativity.

In particular, early man's religious interpretations of the environment show a deep need to make worlds and to assist nature's continuity, a need to dramatize and act out man's intuitions of his relations with nature. The strength of this impulse bears a striking resemblance to the striving of the child to create his own world image. However, we should never equate the adult primitive with the child, for a child is neither adult nor primitive man. A child is a human being, whose development is regulated by the meanings of nature imparted to him by the culture of his particular period in history, the particular mode in which he is taught to see and know himself in time and space.

At one level of organization, this projective behavior is referred to as narrative or story; at another level, which evokes greater breadth and depth in time perspectives, it is identified as history. In this sense the roots of the human sense of history can be said to have emerged from the function of individual nervous systems. History in the spectrum of mind's relations with nature includes, at one extreme, self-history or autobiographical recall, which provides access to the earliest and most finite incidents. At the opposite extreme, mind continues to travel in search of further and further reaches of nature's history and biological evolution; thus biological development and cultural evolution become aspects of cosmic events.

FIVE

The Biocultural Continuum

In ACTUALITY we cannot know anything about ourselves or the world without making comparisons with forms other than the self. This comparison begins at the level of immediate perception and proceeds into the realm of thought and ideas. Though ultimately symbolized thinking reaches higher and higher levels of abstraction, all knowledge nevertheless begins in sensory experience. Mind must retain some awareness of its own physical and anatomical—that is to say, experiential—routes to higher levels, not only in the interest of accuracy and actuality, but also of mental health.

The very act of perception, as well as thinking in terms of culturally framed meanings, enforces this comparative design on learning even in early childhood. We tend to overlook the profound significance of these earlier phases of cognition because of an overemphasis on knowledge as a purely intellectual achievement.

It is generally accepted today that there are three phases of childhood. The first is infancy, with its particular human problem of dependency, which lasts approximately until the fifth or sixth year. The second period is that which Freud called "latency" (referring, however, only to the state of sexual drives), when the bodily self and the powers of speech have normally been brought

53

to a state of full usefulness and equipoise. This period lasts approximately until the age of twelve, when the third phase, the singular human phenomenon of puberty and adolescence, erupts, and instinct once again produces drastic needs and desires. Curiously, it is the infantile characteristic of childhood that returns in this final phase of growing up to interrupt and interfere with the emerging adult.

Because adolescence is dramatic and violent, and because the gifts of the child in the halcyon period of latency are largely non-verbal and can only be accounted for in later recollection, singularly little effort has been made to understand the creative process at this middle stage. There are also subtler and less valid reasons for the neglect of the latency period. For one, the child's paedo-morphic sensibility and intelligence pose a very real threat to many adults. For another, the child's withdrawal into a more con-solidated ego identity has been chiefly examined, psychologically speaking, from the entirely negative point of view of the develop-ment of "defenses." The remarkable cognitive powers deriving from the attitude of the child in this period—when he is poised, so to speak, halfway between inner and outer worlds (a poise so apparent even in the art of children in this phase that Victor Lowenfeld[49] has called it the "x-ray period")—have been neg-lected. The richness and variety of the observations and intuitions of the child at this time, differing in kind from latent instinctual knowledge, during both this period and the infantile stages, have passed unnoticed. I suggest, however, that latency is, in fact, a period in which latent and subliminally experienced images are active but unformulated, awaiting "release" into the wholeness of culturally meaningful expression.

Thus it would appear that although Freud's classification refers only to latent sexual drives, the term "latent" may be more richly interpreted if applied in a wider sense to include other types of "half-knowledge" upon which the individual draws when thinking or perceiving intuitively, not only in this particular period, but throughout life. This period remains the basic phase of develop-ment of human levels of dynamic thought during the whole of life,

in contrast to the period of our infancy, which must be transcended, domesticated, and, in part, repressed. Latent knowledge
is half-formed but subliminal, as is latent learning in animals.

To be sure, between the ages of six and seven the overt creativity of the early years diminishes in output, but the child
achieves an ever greater degree of mastery over the body as an
instrument; problems of organization are thus centered on the
development of personality. During the latency period the aver-
age child is, therefore, an easier, more pleasant person to live with
than is the unrestrained infant or the tempestuous adolescent. The
early sense of his own identity has been established. Psychological
weaning has proceeded to an extent that permits true awareness
of three- and four-dimensional realities. These possess the child's
imagination and carry him into a deepening world image. He is,
in fact, in love with the universe. That is to say, he wants to possess the whole world as his theater of perception.

From a postural viewpoint, he knows himself in the round.
Moreover, the control of body motion and mental activity is now
more clearly within his grasp, for language has become an instrument enabling him to order perceptual experience while also
giving him the power to perceive analogies in verbal terms. This
comparative work in turn gives motion to thought by adding
verbal metaphor to the child's method of learning and creating.
Language imposes pattern and sequence on the flux of mental
experience, and the child senses the need of having a "history," as
well as the need to participate in that history, which is the story
of the world around him. Again, in this sense, language is behavior, a form of patterned energy that enables the child to metabo-
lize his perceptions of the external world.

Most significant is the fact that the specific psychological distance, the discontinuity between self and parents, now has
supreme value as the area in which the child's own creativity is
all-important. In addition, cultural explanations give depth to participation in the world and form to the child's identity.

Despite his continued dependence on the nourishment of love,
the child has an intense need for psychological separation and

complete weaning. This produces an attitude that is much too frequently overexplained as defensiveness. There is, of course, a
large measure of truth in this explanation, but it is usually taken
to refer to defense of the secrecy of fantasy, with its many bodily
implications. I believe, however, that the child's purpose and attitude are to a large extent directed toward preserving the self as
separate—a species in himself. To grow and to know are equated
within the immediate need to create a world of form and meaning
as a survival function, while sexual activity remains unproductive,
although sensed and expected as a future goal.

Therefore the striving toward speciation, found throughout natural history, has culminated in the biocultural nature of the individual human being. Because of the prolonged period of human
childhood and the special irritability (in the biological sense,
commonly described as "sensitivity") of the human nervous
system, the energies of the body as an ecosystem have been
extended into communication systems and into the making of perceptual worlds as a continuity of evolutionary phenomena. The
child's body, highly eroticized and sensitized by nurture and
touch, adds to its total organization the tool we term "mind"; the
child fills in the distance between the self and the objects of desire
with *imagined* forms. This psychological distance between self
and universe and between self and progenitors is the locus in
which the ecology of imagination in childhood has its origin.

Close observation of purpose in the microcosm of the child's
constructive and creative play and play art reveals quite clearly
that self-knowledge and a sense of identity are achieved only by
means of interplay between the organism and its total environment and that all "knowing" emerges progressively at each level
of organization, from tactile systems and functional relations with
environment on up to semantic meaning and language systems—
man's basic method of organizing a spatiotemporal cosmos. Mind
as the highest level of organization of the body's behavior displays
a continuous search for the satisfaction we call "consciousness."
Like perception in all animals, consciousness in humans is "appetitive" behavior.

In Stanley Cobb's neurophysiological definition of consciousness, the comparative pattern of cognition is outlined as
"'awareness' of environment and of self,"[50] while consciousness is
described as a function of nervous systems. Learning and perceiving must, therefore, always have been a seeking of comparisons of
so-called inner and outer worlds, providing infinite possibilities for
further exploration and reinterpretation. This process can be recognized as the source of cultural evolution.

Culture is learned behavior with a biological basis, not only in
the body's capacity to learn, but in the appetite to learn function-
ally, perceptually, and ultimately linguistically. Cultural attitudes,
gestures, and assumptions—negative as well as positive—are also
assimilated nonverbally; but the development of the child's
humanity—that is, the development of the child's ethical sensibilities and the separation of behavior from the immediacy of animal
impulse—takes place within the ethos of human dialogue, which
includes tone and mood as a part of semantic meanings. The child
also "reads" behavior perceptually, including gesture and tone,
long before the structural aspects of language are significant to
him.

Although his tools are cultural, the child's modeling impulses,
perceptual and manual, appear to be spontaneous and biologically
innate. These impulses are instinctive and inventive, while the
child's materials are in a strict sense "natural." Being artifact, as
such, is not the essential nature of any object. The natural proper-
ties of an artifact—its shape, color, and especially its texture and
potential use—are the reality, along with the identity.

Looked at in this way, the child's world making in play is a
learning process, a structuring of increasingly complex gestalten,
both perceptual and linguistic, in a cultural transcendence of biological levels. This process begins in the child's very earliest experimental play with his own body, which Erikson has described,
poetically and yet scientifically, as "autocosmic play."

On this basis, it is possible to sustain the view that the child
does not merely grow but *evolves* out of nature into culture.
Although his biological powers and potentialities do undergo proc-

esses of maturation—processes enabling each individual to direct his energies toward recognized cultural purposes—the child does not simply mature spontaneously on human levels.

Raymond Ruyer[51] has analyzed the differences between the animal *Umwelt* and the perceived cosmos in which man "knows" that he lives. Ruyer finds that knowledge of this difference is necessary to an understanding of the nature of man. Ruyer sees man as a religious animal, living in a universe that was originally religiously conceived as beyond him, while the animal lives in a physiologically experienced domain within "instinctive valences" that "agree" with the animals' organic capacities for response. This argument implies that the human step from valence to value, from the perceptual response of the nervous system to value systems in the universe of discourse, is a true transcendence from biological levels into symbolic systems, into the metaphorical ways of knowing the world. "From a tool at the service of the organism, which it was," consciousness "becomes the perception of a truly external world and, through it, of a transcendental world" (pp. 43-44).

Ruyer also acknowledges aesthetic order in nature:

> From organic art, from the instinctive aesthetics of animals to the art of human culture; from implicit anatomical knowledge manifested by the instinct to scientific knowledge; from the parental instinct to maternal love; from organic technique to conscious technique; from the pseudo-ritual of specific behavior to the authentic ritual of human behavior; from the vital domain to the universal world—the transition is always the same, and it is possible to define with precision the nature of this transition or this inversion.[52]

When it comes to human life, perception is transcended through translation into language; experience of environment becomes thought about environment as knowledge becomes semantic. But at the basis of all perception there remains the physiological drive to organize temporal and spatial relations into meaningful, manageable form and sequence. Unmediated vision is hence not abolished but remains as a part of man's formative impulse. This is most clearly demonstrated in the realms of art, but can, I think, also be observed at its origin in the life of every child. For the child is born clean of the culture, as John Dollard[53] has noted, and we are now aware that no part of culture is innate or biologically transmitted; each and every child is therefore obliged to begin by creating his own world image, translating his innate biological cognitive "equipment" into cultural terms.

This process is a far more remarkable phenomenon than we are apt to realize unless we are especially conscious of the variations in meaning of common language to which every child is exposed. Although the child is dependent on feedback from the environment as a measure of possible future activities, in order to learn in cultural terms he must transcend the immediacy of response of the nervous system so as to achieve his birthright in the world of metaphoric language. Realizing the enormity of this step, Norbert Wiener, who can be described as the father of cybernetics, exclaimed, "It is a miracle that children do learn."[54]

It must be emphasized that, like Wiener, I refer here to the child's ability to learn to think, a process that begins before the child can deal with ethics or morals but is synchronized with a passionate interest in testing the limits of the behavior of things. Wiener reminds us that machines, however ingenious, are not miraculous. They are human inventions and as such are extensions of the mind and nervous system of man that have profoundly affected the processes of perceptual differentiation and cognitive evolution. But the ascendence out of biological nature into human culture achieved by the individual child is a miracle that cannot be entirely explained as resulting from the power to learn, for it also depends on a child's ability to absorb and eventually to *give* the energy of love. Without this step in development a child becomes autistic, egocentric, and solipsistic; the only world he knows is his own. He is encased within his body and image, and only dim echoes of the outer and social world reach his mind. Fantasy rules reality, and the imagery of his perceptions and sensations of inner and outer worlds lacks all agreement with the norms of knowledge as culturally understood.

The passionate need of every child to name and to know the outer world as the road to full humanity has never been more clearly demonstrated than in the case of Helen Keller.[55] It was not simply that her remarkable awakening occurred as a result of learning to spell words and name things; the full realization of what language does for every person (beyond mere communication) did not come to her until after she recognized that verbal images were linked by motion in time, giving her the power to think and to manage syntactically disordered temporal and spatial experiences.

Despite the previous benign effects of the process of learning to identify objects within an ethos in which love and discipline were blended, the unmanageable disorder and frustration of being enclosed within her own body continued to rise, driving Helen's destructive impulses to dangerous extremes of behavior. But when Annie Sullivan introduced her to the motion of the well water flowing over her "linguistic" hand, the linking of images with the words being spelled to her created awareness of the continuity of knowledge in language systems. The backlog of latent learning awaiting formulation joined the sudden sense of power to create form. Information from the environment flowed in and began the nourishment of her hungry spirit. "Upon that day," she wrote later, "my soul was born." The power to organize and to create continuities in speech opened up the evolutionary sense of a future in time. Her sense of identity as an ego–world unity, in which she could play the role of creator, set in motion that richness of response to man and nature which makes a fully human being.

In the multicellular structure of the human organism, blood, bone, flesh, and nerve form a composition of cells that is the bodily self. We are compositions being performed—to paraphrase Portmann[56]—and this permits a scoring that can be recorded technically at differing levels and rhythmical rates, such as heart, pulse, or metabolic action patterns. But at the level of culture, both rhythm and form are translated and transformed into cultural systems of meaning.

If perception is a first-order drive in evolution, as Thorpe maintains, and if, as I maintain, each individual is a biocultural species in himself, it follows that perception in childhood is generic and creative until cultural interpretation assumes a wider and deeper control of meaning.

It is clear that during the years of latency the biology of human personality is in a highly developmental state. Differentiation in the use of language enables the child to weave wider webs with which to net the multiplicity of meanings recorded in perception. Biocultural self-increase is at its height as wonder leads attention to the variety of materials and objects of the world around the child. To repeat, the will to learn by exploration and the need to equate this learning with growth is at its height, yet the child's drive toward worldmaking is still personal. His creativity is still generic and, therefore, poetic in the sense of being highly original. At this stage in life history the strictly human phenomenon of personal evolution becomes an established condition. It is still open, however, to the winds of chance or the loss of personal will power, especially within social conditions that enervate or destroy the compassionate intelligence that is our true humanity.

SIX

The Ecology of Individuality

WHAT WE CALL "insight" is that perception of relations enabling the perceptual structuring of forms in space by animal species. This process expands in human cognition and recognition and is carried forward by the plasticity of perceptual response of the human nervous system. It follows that plasticity of perceptual response in man is greater than that of any other animal species. This is especially true in childhood. This plasticity varies, however, from individual to individual, ranging from excessive malleability to extreme rigidity. High-precision work of the intellect may be accompanied by rigidity of world view, narrowness of interest, and impoverishment of human relationships. Excessive plasticity and malleability of response can, on the other hand, become an *embarras de richesses* and induce a loss of identity (a loss of boundaries between self and world) producing the condition known as schizophrenia. Thus, genius (beyond the early stages) and mental illness are never very far apart. Adult genius carries with it a penalty of suffering accompanying the hypersensitivity of an organism in which the compounded forces of the entire evolutionary history continue to press for expression in novelty of form.

Although we are here concerned mostly with generalized comparisons between the natural genius of the child and the type of adult genius whose productions carry the human spirit forward, we do need to come to grips with the problem of providing outlets for the drive to be productive at adult levels, if we are to stem the tides of mental and spiritual illness.

If wonder is the origin and cause of knowledge, as countless thinkers who have never read Plato continue to note, the attitude of wonder must derive from this very plasticity of response. Such responsiveness itself derives initially from what is known, in biological terms, as "irritability," a fundamental characteristic of living matter. Although the image of irritability in human behavioral responses has purely negative connotations, biologically irritability refers to the sensitivity of "touch systems" of organisms far below the level of those possessing nervous systems. For instance, the leaves of the plant turning toward the stimulation of light, which results in photosynthesis, is in biological terms a display of irritability. Irritability is indeed an adaptive mechanism so strangely resembling feeling in human reactions that one is obliged to pause and consider what is meant by "feeling" as contrasted with "emotion." For our present purposes, however, we oversimplify and assume that feeling indicates an organic, tactile reaction, while emotion implies mobility and direction of complex feeling at another level of organization.

If irritability, as a biological term, is another word for sensitivity in plants, animals, and man, we must note that in human life irritability and sensitivity produce negative behavior as well as creative, formative behavior. If human nature is in some ways an exaggeration of all nature, it is not surprising to find that irritability is characteristic of that exaggeration of human nature we call genius. So it must be recognized that misdirected use of this responsiveness of the ordinary child and the uncommon adult can be highly destructive. It is the goal and purpose of inventiveness that determine the value of the productions of genius.

The emptiness and absurdities in life, so highly emphasized by many of our contemporary artists, may be, and often are, genuine and original expressions of human anguish. If the condition they expose is not remedied by human inventiveness, those aesthetic and dramatic statements may spell the ultimate extinction of humanity in man. Therefore, we must consider the development of the child as it relates to the psychosocial health of the individual and the society. And, since this relationship is an ecological one in the truest sense, we must further explore the relationship between man and nature.

The animation of the body, its biochemical tides, represent the enabling forces of the person-as-it, the level of organization of the self from which the desire to create and to continue growth may be said to stem—that is to say, if we do not deny a body–mind continuity either philosophically or biologically. Such a concept would seem to be much less an a priori or mystical explanation of knowledge than the assumption that the human intellect is a phenomenon totally disconnected from nature and the body.

Intellectual content is certainly more than biological, but the materials with which the mind works are nature's materials. In the hypothesis presented here, the action patterns of the intellect follow biological action patterns, but the forms these actions produce are more than natural, for they have evolved from the minds of individual human beings in interaction with their total environment. Language has enabled man to transmit the form-creating behavior of many individual minds, transcend animal levels of meaning, and create perceptual worlds rich in spiritual value.

The idea that we project meaning upon nature fails entirely to explain how we arrive at our capacity to predict and prefigure natural events, animate nature-as-it in the shape of working models and refined machines, or produce animation even in the "still" image of the plastic arts—our ability, in fact, to continue nature's work of transformation and metamorphosis into a hierarchical continuum of related forms. For it must be reiterated again and again that tools and language also continue to evolve, but only through the instrument of man's mind within his body. Perhaps when we arrive at a full realization that the body is an instrument and a tool, and that the created tool or instrument, whether technical or linguistic, is but an extension of the body, we shall be freer to create and to live dramatically within those situations that express high concepts of transcendence.

Literature, as well as the very language of both the sciences and the arts, today supports the idea that, contrary to the belief that to know oneself is to develop a stable and balanced personality, it is indeed only through creating and recreating perceptual worlds in a continuous interaction or communication between the bodily self and the environment that we achieve and maintain an identity of our own and are at home within our own uniqueness and enforced psychological detachment.

Although the worldmaking of both artist and child is original and generic, this behavior can also be described as a search for existing "laws that permit forms to appear." Worldmaking is learning in the widest sense, but it is also an adaptation to environment as nature, a search for higher levels of synthesis of self and world drawn from the recognition that outer and inner worlds are interdependent aspects of reality, rather than independent states. This recognition is not of necessity an intellectual concept. It can be, and is, continually acted out as a form of aesthetic logic, an innate organic extension of nature's lawful forces that create and operate our own organisms.

Although the Greeks intuitively grasped the relationship of body and cosmos, and regarded the achievement of harmony in this relationship (which included ideas of education and health) as the highest form of social philosophy, this awareness could not extend into medical research in its contemporary form until technical instruments and the vocabulary of the physicist evolved to present levels.

The Greek metaphorical (comparative) way of knowing the world produced a language and an ethos that emphasized the continual interplay between person and universe, the total bodily self as a harmonious counterpoint between body and cosmos. Consequently, Greek philosophy and medicine took the form of a method or *techné* of behavior at many cultural and social levels, more particularly in the form of a philosophy of health. Greek imagination was, therefore, quite consciously ecological and has supplied us with the basis of our contemporary terminology in this field of thought.

When medical philosophy, education, and creativity are openly united, the whole process of education tends to be directed toward creative goals and purposes. It is as if when medicine becomes the highest form of social philosophy (while of necessity remaining firmly linked to the body's needs and functions) the wisdom of nurture permeates all levels of human ecology, even if only in latent or unstated form.

From this viewpoint the history of thought becomes not only a documentation of many journeys of the human spirit toward higher realities, but also the documentation of man's emergence into outer reality and a deepening world image, an emergence into the world of nature, where more and more the ecological laws must guide the spirit because the arts and sciences overlap in an increasingly conscious cooperation. Art as illusion has no place in this world view:

> The landscape and the language are the same,
> And we ourselves are language and are land.[57]

In this statement Conrad Aiken draws upon the Chinese perceptual pattern of nature's interaction with human nature in order to illustrate man's ancient intuitive awareness of a unity; but equally he reflects the human sense of apartness and discontinuity that creates the psychological distances that must be filled with meaning. The poem continues:

> What is this "man"? How far from him is "me"?
> Who, in this conch shell locked the sound of sea?
> We are the tree, yet sit beneath the tree,
> among the leaves we are the hidden bird,
> We are the singer and are what is heard.[58]
>
> . . . .
>
> It is the alchemy by which we grow
> It is the self becoming word, the word
> becoming world. And with each part we play
> we add to cosmic *Sum* and cosmic sum.[59]

Human nature is somewhat like an exaggeration of all of nature; the importance to the individual animal of interaction within a social continuum becomes increasingly sharply defined as we continue our ascent of the tree of life, while the identity of the individual becomes ever more significant, until in human life the singleness of psychological identity becomes of supreme significance to the health of the whole body–mind sequence. This identity depends equally on a social continuum and a bounded image of the self on the one hand and, on the other, a psychological discontinuity between the self and "otherness," both natural and human.

The concept of man implicit, although not elaborated, in Freud's discoveries and in subsequent use of his theories is essentially that although man is an animal, it is not natural to be human. This recognition is a twentieth-century elaboration of Wordsworth's nineteenth-century intuition that our human nature is not a punctual presence but a spirit living in time and space and far diffused. It is difficult, in fact, to see why this image is not self-evident. Ethologists now find that lower forms of animals tend also toward exploratory behavior and must adapt individually to environment, but no single animal can transcend its perceived world or transmit to its descendants any individualized external record of its special adaptation. Yet today every human being, to a greater or lesser extent, performs this particular kind of transcendence, and more often than not leaves behind some oral or documentary account of at least some part of his experience, whether it is significant or insignificant to the historical meaning of his time. Recognizing this situation, biologists at present indicate that human development does transcend all other behavior in nature, but they do not look at the problem in the light of the axiom that it is not natural to be human, seemingly because, as scientists, they have no word for that which is beyond nature. As philosophers of science, however, these same men are outspokenly in search of such terms as "parabiological" or "supraorganic," meaning supranatural or above nature, in order to identify man's variation as a cultural being.

Freud's concept of the effect on human personality of envy and concern about sexual power is but one expression of a fundamental human need for those complexes of physical and physiological powers that stem from nature's energies and are transformed at cultural levels into the tools of individual development. The concept that the individual's creation of a world image is the central drive toward human learning (as adaptation to the environment) brings out the ecological pattern of give and take, not only between inner and outer world, but also between past and present as the "autobiographical" search for futurity. This world image, which "they half create and what perceive" (to recall Wordsworth in *The Prelude*),[60] can then be seen as modified and complicated by the highly sensitive problems of structuring a sexual personality and an ego. The pressure of the desire to maintain a controlling position over this domain is a compound of the image of the body and the roles acted out by the self.

Creative urges, however, are motivated not only by need for sublimation, but also by the developmental strivings of the total psychosomatic self. All living is continual learning and adaptation, without which we fall into what Freud termed "repetition compulsion." Man's mind, representing the upper level of functioning of the whole organism, is as dependent as the body on a continual metabolic refueling from the environment. Furthermore, to record or give external shape to any part of personal experience is to see oneself in some degree extended into outer reality. Even a newspaper item produces a feedback and a startled pleasure in "I am this, and this is me." Even in the simplest day-to-day activities, the experience of being oneself, a "circular causal system" in one's ecology, with the capacity to add forms or to change the very shape and nature of the environment, is in itself a far more creative process, with a much more profound meaning for human beings, than is generally conceded.

In the world of adults (and often in uncurbed conditions in childhood) the magic of the child's play with power turns easily into emotional imperialism, a desire for supremacy. This state of mind is then all too easily disguised as skill and superiority difficult to analyze or to treat reductively, partly because like Hamlet we do recognize in ourselves that "god-like capability and reason" and tend to believe (as indeed we should) that it is not meant to "fust in us unused." Yet here again, I venture to think, new and deeper knowledge of the meaning of childhood in the development of personality, culture, and society can come to our rescue.

The important point is that Freud's method of reductive analysis has provided us with instruments for the debunking of false metaphor and false pride that enable us to rationalize our irrational, antihuman, or subhuman impulses and desires. However, in psychoanalysis we find an attitude or condition somewhat similar to that prevailing when concentration on conditions or objects in the environment is too narrowly focused, thus upsetting the balance of the ecology (which we "sometimes call nature," as R. Buckminster Fuller[61] describes it).

True learning is a response to a stimulus which evokes appetitive behavior, resulting in expansion of ego strength and personal identity. Because effective therapy produces reduction of aggressive tendencies, creative drives tend to be released into action. New adaptations to the external world are creatively expressed. These expressions in turn tend to become a creative stimulus or feedback to the self, and personal evolution continues. But I believe this process can take place only when experience of the world and man is informed by compassionate intelligence. If adaptive modification of behavior is too narrowly confined within self-interest, and does not spread out into a wider and more generous world view, the process of understanding, the expansion into metaphoric evolution which expresses this enlargement of empathy and transcendence of the self, fails to occur. The disturbance of ecological balance in the natural world follows upon individual behavior that is unduly limited to self-interest when mind dwindles or becomes rigidly fixed for lack of mental nourishment and spiritual exercise.

The most important contribution of psychoanalysis in its present form is its effectiveness as releaser of intuitive processes. The freeing of latent memories of experience into creative patterns of perception and expression permits the formation of an extraordinary variety of new insights about the world as well as man. Release of bodily energy from inner conflict then tends to turn toward further exploration of the outer world, and the ability to extrapolate from insight, constructively and in a sense even predictively, is restored. In our present changing image of nature and man, interpretation of nature and of man's place in nature becomes an essential part of therapy as well as the adaptive behavior we try to induce through education.

Analysis of any type presumes that some new and different synthesis is needed and will follow. An analysis of past experience that turns the individual in upon the self in prolonged recollection, reaching down to instinct, puts us in touch with biological memory and the very roots of human nature. The return journey of necessity requires a reorganization of a new adaptation or synthesis of self and world. As our human adaptations are cultural, psychotherapy in general assumes that new cultural syntheses will follow new insight and new acceptance of the self. This type of cultural adaptation does occur as a result of effective psychotherapy—therapy being no more, no less than renewed adaptive learning. But such adaptation and modification of behavior comes about almost "inadvertently" (in the very sense that Fuller uses this term in referring to man's present attitude toward his own inventive manipulation of nature's materials).

From this standpoint, Berenson's account of his "second awakening" provides a most striking example of both method and spontaneity in the search for reality. With systematic honesty Berenson found that he needed a test of his technique of aesthetic discrimination, the perception of living value in art. The "test" came when one morning he was

> gazing at the leafy scrolls carved on the door jambs of S. Pietro outside Spoleto, suddenly stem, tendril, and foliage became alive, and, becoming alive, made me feel as if I had emerged into the light after long groping in the darkness of initiation. I felt as one illumined, and beheld a world where every outline, every edge and every surface was in relation to me, and not, as hitherto, in a merely cognitive one.[62]

The effect of this experience was profound, for Berenson lost his doubts about the actuality of the subjective aspect of these exploratory experiences and found that, by assuming an attitude of recall of primary elements and levels in perception, an "open-system" attitude, he could experience and recreate the quality and value of form-producing processes in nature as well as in art. Furthermore, as he noted, he became his own artist when perceiving the realities of the natural world. His sensibilities had been educated by the arts until art had made nature and reality more perceivable. The inanimate or "still" image in the plastic arts had become animate, and nature-as-process had become mentally accessible. Berenson points out that "the world outside ourselves, the non-ego, that stretches before and around us, is a script we have to learn to read."[63] But the ability to see afresh, to revise, review, and reinterpret this same world in a continuous state of growth and change depends on the individual capacity to "dissolve" experience to primary levels of motion, color, and form in the ever-changing context of time and space and so to reorder and rebuild new and different forms, to multiply the worlds we live in. The primary perceptual ingredients are universal, but interpretation of meaning can never be absolute. Language and thought—that is, organized perceptions and intellectual patterns—change as knowledge develops, producing new meaning and new scripts, which evolve out of the older interpretations.

Thorpe, in his discussion of perception, emphasizes that perceptually speaking, nothing enters the receptor systems of the body, even the eye, except energy—radiant energy, chemical energy, and so forth. The organizing processes of the perceiving nervous system create the forms perceived. In his great and beautiful work *On Growth and Form*, a seminal book for both scientists and artists, D'Arcy Thompson says that "the form of an object is a diagram of forces. . . . The waves of the sea, the little ripples on the shore, the sweeping curve of the sandy bay . . . the shape of the clouds, all these are so many riddles of form, so many problems of morphology."[64] Animate and inanimate are subject to the same type of analysis. "Cell and tissue, shell and bone, leaf and flower, are so many portions of matter, and it is in obedience to the laws of physics that their particles have been moved, moulded and conformed."[65] All are perceived and may be analyzed as cosmic events, for "the heavens are formed of like substance with the earth" (how important is that one word, *with*), and "the movements of both are subject to the selfsame laws" and all of these riddles "the physicist can more or less easily read and adequately solve."[66]

However, Thompson continues, the term "force" as used by the physicist "is a term as subjective and symbolic as form itself." Most significant of all, "the state, including the shape or form, of a portion of matter is the resultant of a number of forces, which represent or symbolize the manifestations of various kinds of energy."[67]

These same laws that hold true of the body of human adult or child must presumably also apply to forms created in art or any other morphogenetic modeling by hand, eye, and mind. The forces of nature that "permit forms to appear" and allow us to think of biological life as a "stream of forms surging up through geological time" must surely also supply the mind with the power to create mentally and projectively in interaction with the forces of the environment. Could this also explain to some extent why we do not know the locus of mind, spirit, or genius and cannot identify energy except, in Thompson's phrase, as the "power to do work"? If the whole body is the tool of mind, can it be that mind is a raising of metabolic body patterns? The suggestion has already been made by Herrick, who notes that "the vital process which generates a conscious experience appears to be due to special kinds of metabolism which differ in some as yet unknown way" from autonomic bodily functions and systems. But, he adds, "There is a step up of pattern here which is similar in principle to that which occurs at the level of inorganic process to that of vital process,"[68] which is surely a form of transcendence, possibly the result of reaching into time and space for the feedback of information from the environment.

Although the suggestion is bold, depth analysis of the biology of perception to the level of temporal and spatial relations and its historical role of perception in evolution brings us to just such a point. These concepts must be regarded in terms of pattern and design in the behavior of nature whether we are concerned with perception, metabolic action, or the fulfillment of form. Nevertheless, the right to extrapolate metaphorically—which we do when we compare the histories of nature and man—is better sought in the literature of analysis of creative perception in the arts and in literature.

Extrapolation in the sciences, however, is of necessity metaphorical; it is also one way of describing biological evolution, because such description can only exist in verbal form. But, when cultural evolution in metaphorical terms is equated solely with the conduct we perceive to be at work in scientific and technological advances, the depersonalizing of man's relations with nature and his fellow human beings assumes highly destructive and alarming proportions. More than anything else, love of nature and love of the child have taught humankind to cultivate mind as well as the garden, to domesticate landscape as well as home and personality. But this thinking belongs to simpler biocultural levels than are allowed for in the present hypnotic attraction for mechanized motion and the conquest of nature. As the environment crumbles and steel and concrete take the place of earth, the spirit may crumble as well. Without the element of spirit, man becomes sheer animal while retaining the cunning of intellect.

According to René Dubos, "The evolutionary development of all living organisms, including man, took place under the influence of cosmic forces that have not changed appreciably for very long periods of time. As a result most physiological processes are still geared to these forces."[69] Medical science attempts to reinforce man's adaptability to his environment by altering and controlling, through medication and surgery, individual variations in the body's use of these cosmic forces. Medical science of necessity relies on ecological design in therapy.

Dubos's observations are of singular value to the present work, for he makes clear that one must think in terms of individual health as successful adaptation to the cosmos as well as to culture and society and that this adaptation is temporal as well as spatial.

> Man's propensity to imagine what does not yet exist, including
> what will never come to pass, . . . most clearly differentiates him
> from animals. The more human he is, the more intensely do his
> anticipations of the future affect the character of his responses to
> the forces of the present.[70]

This reasoning leads to the knowledge that health of personality
depends on personal creativity, because in the midst of responding to stimuli and adapting to them, each person tries to achieve
some self-selected end. By medical definition, health and "acts of
personal creation" are inextricably interwoven.

Medically speaking, according to Dubos, "The sort of 'mutuality' that exists between organisms and their normal environment
has become a requirement for physiological and psychological
well-being."[71] This mutuality is best expressed by the word "ecology."

The necessity and benefit of such mutuality is shown by the
case history of Alice,[72] a child surrounded by empty psychological space, with no incentive to cross this distance, no exploratory
need, no creative drive that would enable her to enter worlds
other than that of her own closed-in self. Deprivation of this pro-
portion led finally to anxieties of many kinds. Disorganization of
body image and world image followed. Alice became seriously ill,
with schizophrenia.

The psychiatrist's long and full account of the starvation of
human relations in Alice's otherwise privileged child-life and adolescence contains a reference to "an inconsistent element in her
history, . . . [a] sea-change which is reported to have occurred
each year during their stay at the family summer home." The psychiatrist's astonishment is evident—he is unable to place this
piece in any particular context in his psychiatric account of Alice's
life history. "It was as if this were an annual Cinderella episode,
sharply distinct from her life." The language of the psychiatrist
touches on the poetic—"a sea-change" and "Cinderella" lift us out
of the realms of observation of pathology into a charmed recognition of the poetics of a child's therapeutic experience of the natural world.

During her treatment, Alice herself turns poet when she relives these times. In a truly Whitmanesque style she immerses herself once again in the imagery of that summer world that flowed in and through her and affected all levels of her relationship with people as well as her general behavior and ways of thinking:

> Big trees, pine trees swishing in the wind. The Mountain, blue and hazy in the distance, grass blowing below like waves on the ocean. Sticky bark, blue jeans, that was Michigan—and tennis, lots of it, every day. Then a cool swim, dive off the dock and the water rushing by, swimming, lying on the raft, picnics on the beach, the Point, singing, and marshmallows, sweet and black.

The lines flow rhythmically and lyrically, and the imagery is intense but concrete, even in the midst of psychosis. As she writes (externalizes) and recalls autobiographically the actuality of eco-logical experiences, she becomes in memory as she was then, briefly each year, a happy, forward-looking child and adolescent:

> Canoes. Water against the paddle pushing ahead, home late, moon on the water, crickets singing, stumbling up the path carrying blankets and Jack giggling, always giggling and having to kiss me. Poor Jack. Michigan and Michigan again, always different, each year it changed—it didn't change, I did, a new me in the same place. Each summer I would wonder what would happen . . . each one with something new, unexpected, exciting, for me to have and to remember, never lose it, always have it, in me, never forget it, just think about it, relive it over and over, love it and keep it, part of me . . . for me, *is me*. (Italics added.)

Body image and world image had conjoined during these experiences, giving a sense of true identity. Even when the sense of movement goes out of control in later lines, the reality of the senses is interwoven with the torrential flow of the imagery of movement—"twisting, revolving, rotating, squirming, wriggling, slithering, snakey . . . water breaking, sliding past, new water passing by, turning white, turning black, turning green, turning blue, going far away, never come back, off to nowhere" and from there on, in the piece quoted, the writing deteriorates, a piteous dissipation of all solidity into shapeless feeling; helpless longing follows, ending on a note of bewildered exhaustion.

The deep need of a child for some experience of the living world is an intuitive part of our ideas of holidays. But our knowledge of what this implies needs to be systematized and tied in with the poetic principle in the mind of man and the heart of childhood as the core of learning. We cannot teach children (or adults) to learn or to love. We can only *release* the power to love, which leads to love of learning.

The child's delight and "intellectual" wonder, the relief from ennui and sickness that adults seek in a change of scene, are equally served by satisfaction of the appetite of nervous systems for fresh stimuli from the environment. As Dubos notes, "experience shows that human beings are not passive components in adaptive systems. Their responses commonly manifest themselves as acts of personal creation. Each individual person tries to achieve some self-selected end even while he is responding to stimuli and adapting to them."[73] Body and mind cannot be separated, for perception by the nervous system must be transcended, organized, and coordinated into the language structure of the culture within which the person lives. Therefore, "Health in the case of human beings means more than a state in which the organism has become physically suited to the surrounding physicochemical conditions . . . it demands that the personality be able to express itself creatively.[74] This, in turn, implies that we must learn to treat creativity in terms of value systems that differ from intellectual achievement yet reinforce positive aesthetic attitudes toward nature and man and our culturally created world imagery.

Although Dubos focuses upon the symbolic activities of man's mind as the ultimate expression of the humanness of human nature, he refers to the necessity of sensory stimulation in childhood as continuing on into the functioning of the nervous system in adult life. So he says that studies in this area are revealing that "development of the nervous system and even mental health depend upon a constant exposure to sensory stimuli and to new experiences."[75]

The body in infancy and childhood is enmeshed in a web of related somatic "anticipations" and neural "expectancies," to use Gesell's terms. The processes of growth and metabolic renewal of tissues must continue as a survival function. Healing and learning are curiously similar problem-solving, form-creating functions; both also involve the organizing of spatiotemporal relations and both are ultimately cosmic phenomena, although expressed in biologically based patterns of behavior.

But before experiences can become meaningful, they must be brought to a state of structure and form. The most purely human activities that produce form and structure are to be found in the iconography of play and art. These are also closest to the immediacy of acts of perception. That it should be necessary for thoughtful educators to insist on direct work with the arts as basic to learning, especially at the elementary and secondary levels, is evidence of a gap in knowledge. The task of retaining one's identity by relating learning to individual patterning of world imagery is a pressing one. On the other hand, although the arts—particularly the plastic arts—are known to be helpful in therapeutic work, it is now understood that the use of painting, modeling, and other manual creative work, although often modifying fear and aggression, cannot alone help a person in isolation to redefine the meaning of his relations with the world. Therapy must take the form of dialogue in which the therapist evokes self-history as narrative sequence within a specific technique of human relationships. But such formal correction is never as effective as spontaneous discovery and learning.

Our new knowledge of the young child's striking ability to learn tends to encourage the fallacies about the supreme role of intellect and the superiority of the memorizing type of intelligence—the type that tends to stimulate competitive parental or communal wishes.

The Autobiography of John Stuart Mill[76] gives a telling illustration of the way exploitation of the intellect can lead to psychological disaster. The example of Mill is particularly fascinating, as it demonstrates the possibility of the expansion of a different order of intelligence in later life if the heart as well as the mind is nourished in childhood by a knowledge that can later be reactivated, thus adding meaning to early cognition derived from sense experience.

The pivotal point in John Stuart Mill's recovery from a serious depression, with its accompanying loss of interest and purpose, came as a result of reading Wordsworth's poems. Despite frequent references, particularly by contemporary philosophers and scientists, to lines or phrases drawn from Wordsworth, it is highly improbable that any such dramatic depth of response to these particular poems could occur in our contemporary ethos. The language and experience of Mill's view of nature in his particular cultural era were sufficiently in agreement with Wordsworth's poems, while at the same time the poet's vision was sufficiently evocative to affect Mill therapeutically.

The primary result was the release of Mill's own childhood memories of sheer sense experience, enabling him to give them order and synthesis and to establish intellectual continuity and a hitherto lacking integration of self and world. Although his sense of wonder had been active, as it is in any child, his energies had been channeled into focusing on the intellectual recordings of other minds, which had little or no relation to his early creative perception of his own world, in particular his experience of the natural world.

Mill was the son of an intellectually ambitious father, himself the son of a petty tradesman; the child's strangely cerebral life seemed guaranteed to break down his personality. Nevertheless, a bond of real affection between father and son served to reinforce Mill's identification with his father and his desire to be like him.

Greek lessons at the age of three were followed by an incredible reading list that continued through boyhood. One reason for the tenacity of Mill's interest lies in the fact that the father was deliberately trying to make the boy into a critical instrument and an extension of his own adult self, a satisfying experience to a small favored child. But, because the boy had not first had the experience of a child's world, the breakdown eventually came.

Concentration on the analytic process in working with adult ideas and an overemphasis on reflection ground to a halt in a mental crisis; in his late twenties Mill suffered a long spell of deep depression.

Mill's response to Wordsworth's poetry was possible because Wordsworth's attitude toward the poignancy and creative power of childhood experience is so soundly based psychologically. Wordsworth's dialectical love affair with nature is so entrenched in the powerful actuality of original childhood experience that the reader's own association with childhood is revived and confirmed in positive, culturally recognized adult form. The effect is to restore to a perceptive reader the right to believe in and make use of his own sensory experience as a child, setting free an inner conviction that the value of common experience is basic to the power to create and to evolve creatively and imaginatively.

Mill claims to have learned from Wordsworth that the (so-called) "passive susceptibilities needed to be cultivated as well as the active capacities and required to be nourished and enriched."[77] The phrase "passive susceptibilities" refers to the intuitive, aesthetic levels of sense experience. In this state of mind, the reading of Wordsworth became the solid ground for a synthesis of himself and the natural world around him. He did not reject or lose the print of his intellectual training, but he realized that "the habit of analysis has a tendency to wear away the feelings: as indeed it has when no other mental habit is cultivated, and the analysing spirit remains without its natural complements and correctives."[78] In fact, Mill is critical of Wordsworth as a poet, but Wordsworth taught him the value of what an ecologist has described as "mental prolepsis"—a casting back into history in order to go forward in time. Man needs to sense a biocultural continuity with nature in order to tap the sources of energy that motivate his own power of creative synthesis.

In terms of this thesis, the development and functioning of the perceiving nervous system, described by Herrick, Coghill,[79] and others as a complementary process of analysis–synthesis, indicates the need for a similarly balanced action pattern in thought. In any effort to think synoptically, these complementary patterns are vital to psychological balance and to the integration of the human organism with the environment.

Wordsworth, like many another autobiographical writer discussing the same theme, specifically denies any value to "childishness." For Wordsworth is not concerned with psychiatric regression or with inner conflicts but rather with the special human power of semantic reduction in memory—the power of reliving, of using a reversal of time in memory in order to dissolve meaning to more directly perceptual levels.

The intelligence of the child during latency is rarely compassionate, but the power of creative perception, and the particular intelligence that accompanies perception at this time of life, survives many kinds of deprivation and many destructive conditions. It is not surprising, therefore, that the seductive power of this temporal period poses its own particular danger to the will to continue to evolve. It impedes the will to emerge four-dimensionally into the larger humdrum world of everyday purpose, which is so essential to psychological development. For the latency period contains, as latent power and purpose, the seeds of the writer's art, the painter's vision, and the explorer's passion. In sum, it contains a true sense of the evolutionary power from which these and all other generic gifts are developed.

No more remarkable illustration of both the perils and the potentialities of this phase of life history can be found than that of the Brontë children's worldmaking in the kitchen of the parsonage at Haworth—a period long misread as a picture of neglected and lonely childhood in bleak, barren surroundings.

Settled around the kitchen table, ministered to by the faithful Tabitha—herself a great teller of tales—Branwell, Charlotte, Emily, and Anne constructed Angria and Gondal, two imaginary environments with euphonious and poetic names. Their world play, initiated by their father's gift to Branwell of a box of toy soldiers, was a typical response of childhood to a population of toy figures transferred and transformed into the rhetoric of play. They created a cast of characters and made "all merely players."

They invented nomenclature for their characters that remained singularly childish, with a babble tone—"Sneaky," "Bravey," "Stumps," "Gravey," and the like—in contrast to the charm of the environmental names, which are comparatively sophisticated and probable. An occasional political or social name, such as the Duke of Wellington, appeared as the children drew apart into their own named provinces and islands. These, however, remained an interactive whole as part of the same world game—a true universe of discourse. The ecological nature of this world can be seen from Emily Brontë's poetic line, "We wove a web in childhood, a web of sunny air." This intuition led Fannie Ratchford to transform the line into *The Brontës' Web of Childhood*,[80] the title of her book.

This world, coupled with their reading, permitted them to test their ideas against reality. So intense was the Brontë children's common endeavor to build on patterns found in the world of social and everyday actualities—such as newspapers and correspondence among all of their special characters, with maps of their special provinces to guide them—that eventually this world play became to each of them more a matter of reality than of fantasy.

The worldmaking of the Brontë children was the product of their imaginative search for reality and not of the more or less predetermined type of wish-fulfillment behavior we call fantasy. As Fannie Ratchford points out, their poetic worlds literally "grew up" or evolved to increasingly higher levels of organization, one stage unfolding into the next until the sequence of plot and personality in Angria and Gondal became the themes of the novels and the poems.

However, with the possible exception of Charlotte, the Brontës never left the psychological phase known as latency. Emily in particular formed an attachment to the wild beauty of the Yorkshire landscape, which held her in thrall to the end of her life. Not one of these intellectually gifted children emerged into the four-dimensional continuum of fully adult life, in a temporal sense. That is to say, as grownups the Brontës remained unable to act out in fully adult form the depth of understanding and insight that they displayed in their projected characterizations. For one thing, they remained unable to achieve fully adult roles at responsible psychosexual levels.

The importance to psychological insight of the example of the Brontës' world play is many-faceted. Biographies and autobiographies demonstrate that group play in large and somewhat isolated families has generated many kinds of creative activity.

The Brontës are an example of the natural genius of childhood in a group stimulated by each other to the point at which each evolved a separate process of creativity to genius level. But a persisting overattachment to the powerful physical level of organization of biological nature, from which imagination as an evolutionary process stems, tends to exaggerate the desire for private worlds, even when such a desire may be aesthetically and artistically expressed at high levels of projection. To some extent every creative person must contend with this problem.

Ultimately, mature purpose, either emotional or cultural, requires recognition of the limits of the self and a capacity, within recognition, for suffering. This, in turn, implies the capacity to perceive creatively despite suffering and awareness of the discontinuity between self and the world.

If we consider mental development as a personal evolution from biological levels through cultural means, the intuitive but latent perceptual discovery made by the child in this exodus into nature as a deepening, evolving world image, is that his knowledge of the real world is organized around his own perception and that he and nature are involved in some common formative purpose.

The child's search for reality now seems to bring the world within his grasp. He senses that he has the power to make world pictures based on a behavioral tactile knowledge of nature's potential behavior (laws). Although this power stems from the physical forces that sustain the posture and behavior of his own organism, it is now the outer world, the power of the universe "striking upon what is found within," as Wordsworth put it, that produces recognition by the responding, recording nervous system and releases the forces of imagination to further inventiveness.

Attitudes toward the child have varied throughout known cultures and civilizations, with varying effects on human behavior and human societies. The lyrical effect of love of the child on the quality of human nature and human culture has been anciently demonstrated in such early expressions, for instance, as the lullabies of very primitive peoples. Such themes stem, however, from love of possession of a biologically created child and from the joy of nurturing the child one has made, whereas our present attitude and position is based on a recognition of childhood as a value system in human culture and personality. Present knowledge that the child's bodily metabolism requires the intake of energy expressed as love, as well as the energy derived from the intake of milk and bread, makes the body the "nursery of the soul."

Parental love has become a medically defined requisite for the health of the infant's body (most specifically, as this kind of loving care relates to the evolving mind), while methods of bestowing this nourishing energy of love are constantly refined and expanded into learned techniques and culturally developed skills. Cultural continuities of biologically conditioned impulse require this shaping influence. The codes and techniques of behavior developed by human cultures have a certain aesthetic, refining, shaping intent, even at very primitive levels. Culture by intention overtly attempts to transcend biological fulfillment of instinctual drives.

In the twentieth century, health of the child and health of societies have been found to be inextricably interwoven. Such knowledge of human nature and human need cannot be confined to Western civilizations, where it has emerged as science, for it has spread and is spreading daily around the highly industrialized world of global economics. Modern medicine and modern concepts of mental health travel faster and further along these industrial pathways and skyways than do any other expressions of culture. Translated into differing concepts in differing cultures, these medical prescriptions for successful living, with their emphasis on the significance and value of childhood, are inter-woven with the instinctual joy of bearing and loving a child, thus bringing their influence to bear upon man's sense of destiny in far corners of the earth.

Although as yet we seem scarcely aware of it intellectually, this contemporary knowledge that childhood is a biologically condi-tioned phase, of special significance to the formation of character structure and personality, introduces a major shift in concepts and in interpretations of the very meaning of history and time. Biolog-ical explanations of man's nature now intensify his knowledge of his relationship with the natural world and deeply affect his exploration of his own destiny. When Freudian psychoanalytic psychology linked Darwinian concepts of evolution with the indi-vidual life history of every human being, this unifying principle, like Keats's "whispering of the leaves, put a girdle around the earth." From then on, all interpretations of human history became obligated to anthropology as the biocultural science of human his-tory as well as in the framework of cultural evolution.

SEVEN

The Evolution of Meaning

A man's life of any worth is a continual allegory.
—Keats, 1819

ALTHOUGH the literature of autobiography is often questioned or regarded with suspicion as a mode of self-justification or outright confession, childhood memories in Eastern as well as Western cultures, in antiquity as well as in the present, contain markedly similar accounts of moments of "vision" that, when deliberately or sometimes accidentally recalled in later life, renew the desire to be creative. These statements deserve far more serious consideration than they have as yet received. The most striking remembrances of this type describe an acute pleasure in the incoming flux of minutiae—the mosaic of immediate sensory experience of the natural world on the one hand, and on the other a sudden exultation and delighted sense of freedom in the vastness of open spaces, namely, time.

In my collection of autobiographical recollections by creative thinkers from many cultures and eras, ranging from a fragment from a sixteenth-century statement by Giordano Bruno[81] and continuing into the present, the writers describe highly similar childhood memories to which they return in order to renew the power and impulse to create.

In these memories the child appears to have experienced both a momentary sense of discontinuity—an awareness of his unique separateness and identity—and a revelatory sense of continuity —an immersion of his whole organism in the outer world of forms, colors, and motions in unparticularized time and space. This type of apprehension is certainly not intellectual. It is often mistakenly thought to be either mystical or totally subjective and irrational; I suggest that it is rational, at least in a limited sense, as a preverbal experience of an aesthetic logic present in both nature's formative processes and the gestalt-making powers and sensibilities of the child's own developing nervous system. Inner and outer worlds are sensed as one in these moments of form-creating expansion and self-consciousness.

These vivid experiences, described retrospectively by adults, appear to be universal and suggest some universal link between mind and nature as yet uncodified but latent in consciousness in intuitive form. For example, minds as far apart and as different in value as Isaac Newton's and Salvador Dali's have been entranced by the image of a child springing joyously over the sands or poised at the edge of the sea:

> I do not know what I may appear to the world; but to myself I seem to have been only like a boy playing on the seashore, and diverting myself in now and then finding a smoother pebble or a prettier shell than ordinary, while the great ocean of truth lay all undiscovered before me.[82]

"Autographed" recollections of the image of the child momentarily suspended in a clarity of unmediated awareness should be valued not merely for their visual charm, but also for their actuality.

The authenticity of verbal accounts of these charmed moments of illumination, which are not confined to visual perception, is attested to by the very simplicity and clarity of the language used to describe them. Ordinary or common-sense experiences of many kinds suddenly assume uncommon value and meaning in the clear light of these luminous verbal recollections of acute experience of the outer world.

Experiences that were inexpressible in verbal form in childhood but were nonetheless closer to body rhythm and process than later formulations of knowledge can be, retain their poetic creative power and are translatable into verbal image and temporal sequence. As in animals, these strata of "latent learning" reappear at a time when some stimulus evokes the memory once more.

We have seen that the child's attitude of hypothetical awareness can be directly related to the concept of an innate principle of expectancy in animal nervous systems. This animal heritage in its human form becomes, I have suggested, a biocultural continuity. In childhood, the cognitive process is essentially poetic because it is lyrical, rhythmic, and formative in a generative sense; it is a sensory integration of self and environment, awaiting verbal expression. The child "knows" or re-cognizes in these moments that he makes his own world and that his body is a unique instrument, where the powers of nature and human nature meet. These very moments are recalled autobiographically by the adult who seeks to renew and reinforce vision and so extend creative powers.

That man's prolonged infancy and childhood is neotenous goes without saying. That during this period of delay the child's learning abilities are phenomenal has only recently been considered to be of much significance, except for highly developed genius or the exceptional child. But if man's humanity is paedomorphic in biological terms, deriving from the reciprocity or mutuality of relations imposed by the needs of childhood upon evolving social ties through millennia, then we can take up the theme of the value to cultural evolution of intelligence in childhood.

Examining statements of adult geniuses about their own childhood and comparing them with references to the child in myths and early religious interpretations of the origins of the world, we note striking resemblances to the world play of the child. In addition, it seems clear that there is and always has been widespread intuitive awareness that certain aspects of childhood experience remain in memory as a psychophysical force—an élan that produces the pressure to perceive creatively and inventively, that is, imaginatively.

Originality and creativity require a basic receptiveness without "any irritable reaching after fact and reasoning," as Keats wrote when describing "negative capability," which permits intuition to actuate novelty of relations in perception or thought.

Yet in order to reach such levels of receptiveness and responsiveness, we must maintain an ability to think reductively and extend our human capacity to allow the mind (like the whole organism) periods of nonsteady states, so that—as in childhood —we may hearken to the language of the body as an information system. Only in this way can we continue to hope to maintain a general adaptiveness to changes in relations with and meaning of the environment. Bacon summarizes this potential "reading" of actuality:

> This is that speech and language which hath gone out to all the ends of the earth, and has not suffered the confusion of Babel—this must men learn, and resuming their youth, become again as little children, and deign to take its alphabet into their hands.[83]

To bring these childhood incidents closer to the cosmic language and thought of our own era, we can draw upon the memories of Pierre Teilhard de Chardin as recorded by Nicolas Corte. Pursuing the pattern of reflexive consciousness of genius as a thought process, de Chardin gives an autobiographical account of his own early passion for matter as "itness," which marked the beginning of his journey into knowledge and remained a talisman —a condensation of experience into symbol, if you will—all his life. He writes, "I was certainly no more than six or seven when I began to feel myself drawn by Matter—or more exactly by something that 'shone' at the heart of Matter." He had, he says, "caught" the usual child's religion from his mother, but this secret preoccupation was an entirely separate kind of "worship." It was worship of iron! He collected a whole series of "idols"—in the country a plow key, in town a metal staple, even shell splinters.[84]

At the age of sixty-nine and famous, de Chardin remembers that "in this instinctive movement which made me truly speaking *worship* a little piece of metal, there was a strong sense of self-giving and a whole train of obligations all mixed up together."[85]

The images common to such memories of childhood appear in his references to the meaning of his experience: for example, his need to "savor" the existence of "my god, iron," in a merger of taste and touch. This is a metaphorical description of a true appetitive behavior in the ethological sense which, as Teilhard himself states, contained all the passions, including knowledge and love itself, but was above and beyond them. From the age of four or five, he notes, he already had "a general cosmic sense (a consistency of the whole)"—a sense of continuity. Hence, research for de Chardin became a form of worship, a knowing through the merging of the self with nature and human nature on the way to God. Regarding the lumps of matter manifested as iron, which he swore never to lose sight of in his search for the "physics of mind," he knew intuitively that there was imbedded in these objects, as in his own organism, a narrative continuity, a history of nature to be unfolded in metaphorical language. He states clearly that the early experience sowed the seeds of his pursuit of cosmic and biological evolutionary history in later life and that his capacity stemmed from these inarticulate roots.

As we have seen, memories of men who have advanced knowledge in the world of science actually contribute some of the most concrete statements about the value of the child's way of perceiving—and this is as true of the cultures of the East as of the West, of the ancient as well as modern world. For instance, the Chinese sage Mencius said, "The wise man retains his childhood habit of mind."[86] Charles Sherrington, writing as a physiologist, reminds us that "to recapture now and then childhood's wonder, is to secure a driving force for occasional grown-up thoughts."[87] I repeat, these direct references to the force of interest engendered by the child's questioning attitude, appearing as they do in the context of works of high scientific and philosophical quality of speculation, should be read not for their charm but their verity. Lorenz states:

Intuition is generally regarded as the prerogative of artists and poets. I would assert that it plays an indispensable role in all human recognition, even in the most disciplined forms of inductive research. Though in the latter the important part taken by intuition is very frequently overlooked, no important scientific fact has ever been "proved" that had not previously been simply and immediately seen by intuitive Gestalt perception. . . . Intuition it was when Kepler first perceived in the complicated epicycles of the planets' apparent movements, the simple regularity of their real orbits, or when Darwin first saw in the intricate tangle of living and extinct forms of life, the convincingly clear Gestalt of the genealogical tree.[88]

Lorenz considers this function of generic recognition to be the probable phylogenetic precursor of conscious abstraction. This ability of perceptual objectivizing and seizing upon constant aspects of a whole (the perception of consonant form) was, Lorenz feels, the great and essential change in function that led to the development of conceptual thought and speech.

These statements are, in fact, not so much extrapolations as reinterpretations of generally accepted descriptions of nature and human nature, expanded to include the logic of present information in the biological and behavioral sciences and extended into a working model of the basis of human culture, beginning in the microcosm of the infant body.

Once again, the contemporary design of ecological thinking offers an explanation of why this pattern of recollection is so valuable to an understanding of the creative process in nature. As Deevey noted, ecology "builds firmer bridges toward the humanities and toward the earth sciences, as well as toward the social and behavioral sciences, than do other kinds of biology."[89]

That the metaphor of evolution as the overall view of history is releasing an ever deepening search for methods of analysis of mind and cosmos, is clearly evidenced by Kenneth Clark's 1954 Romanes lecture.[90] In the famous Sheldonian Theatre at Oxford, where Darwinian controversy reached a peak in the defeat of Bishop Wilberforce by Thomas Huxley, Clark turned his attention to the sources of creativity in childhood experience in a lecture entitled "The Moment of Vision."

The lectures were established in 1891 by George John Romanes, an English biologist who was a friend of Darwin's.

Darwin had encouraged him to apply the theory of natural selection to mental evolution and to psychology, and the lectures follow this pattern. But the Clark lecture turns toward the evolution of creativity in the arts in the individual personality. Clark's analysis leads to a consideration of the role of perception in human development and to the illumination—that is, the light suffused into the mind by wonder—in the commonplace experience of childhood. Clark argues that this sense of wonder can only be synthesized in adult imagination after further intercourse with literature or art. As in the case of the remarkable evolution of the Brontë children's play world into novels and poems, the examples cited by Clark have evolved from the commonplace world of experience in childhood, which has, however, its moments of vision of illuminated recognition.

In his introductory words Clark notes that "a more explicit title would have been 'The Moment of Intensified Physical Perception'" and that he is "not going to talk about vision in the metaphorical sense."[91] The removal of actual visual immediacy from the vocabulary of perception is most fortunate, for it leaves us with the unmediated vision of the total perceiving nervous system, the total bodily self in childhood. Clark adds, "We may not experience these illuminations very often in our busy adult lives, but they were *common* in our childhood, and given half a chance we could achieve them still" (italics added).[92]

In childhood "everything is observed to an almost intolerable extent," as Pasternak has written autobiographically. "Lamps, typists, doors and galoshes, clouds, moon, snow. Terrible world." Hence, the need to learn and the need to discriminate, name, and classify is overwhelmingly strong. Pasternak tells us how, in his own case, "in a mode of feeling reminiscent of Gumilev's 'sixth sense', nature was revealed to a ten-year-old. How botany appeared as his first passion in response to the five-petaled persistence of the plant. How names, sought out according to the classified text, brought peace to eyes of flowers that seemed filled with scent, in their unquestioning rush towards Linnaeus, as if from nonentity to fame."[93]

The image of the "five-petaled persistence of the plant" combines Pasternak's adult knowledge of the biological concept of persistence of form in time and the verbal stabilizing of the child's aesthetic experience of creating form with mind and eye. The need of the child, the poet, and the scientist to give perception a semantic persistence in thought is dramatized. The creative history of man's work as scientist is compressed in the childlike "rush towards Linnaeus" and stands for the search by both poet and scientist for evolutionary futurity of the individual and the race. In following the pattern of mental prolepsis as a moving to and fro between past and present in his own life history, Pasternak also reawakens for us a sense of Linnaeus's discovery of the need for method in the classification of experience in any step forward in cognitive evolution. There is a logic in Pasternak's childhood joy in finding a method of ordering and naming the parts of the world he shares with living things, the joy of discovering order and logic in nature's aesthetics.

Thus, the truly creative adult contrives to raise primary, less highly organized but deeply intuitive, aspects of awareness closer to consciousness with all the respect of the artist for the beauty and simplicity of his own primary materials. In effect, this process is the reverse of intellectual abstraction, when rational thought employs symbols and symbolic systems as basic material. Yet it is not any less important and useful to intellectual effort. Nor is it a passive proceeding, for it necessarily involves participation in nature's ongoing activities; it is a relation-seeking effort, with a formative intent and ultimately is dependent on the shaping power of intellect.

The gifted person—the genius, if you will—does tend to regress perhaps more often than others less gifted. But every human being frequently regresses to lower, less developed levels of behavior and purpose. And the psychobiological pressures to which the adult genius is exposed are exaggerated by the powerful drive toward the outer formulation of his vision in the discipline through which his genius is expressed. The point is that it is not the moments of regression that empower actual creativity—an idea often proposed in psychoanalytic studies of creativity. It is the capacity for returning reductively to the use of universals, to the "materials" that furnish human beings with the power to create imagery, that inspires adult creativity. In childhood this behavior is innate and spontaneous, the normal process a child employs when fulfilling his basic appetite for knowledge. Wordsworth writes:

> Such, verily, is the first
> Poetic Spirit of our human life;
> By uniform control of after years
> In most abated or suppressed, in some,
> Pre-eminent till death.[94]

The dual fallacies of implied permanent maturity and permanent norms, which are now embedded in the medical and psychological sciences, cut us off from recognition of the continuity of childhood potential. These fallacies are errors in the use of concepts of time, which subsequently produce errors in ideas of value.

Creative evolution, as understood in this work, consists in the achievement of richer and more creative relations of the total (but individual) organism with its total environment. Although this evolution into knowing may occur at nonverbal levels or develop within the discovery of the power of words, the final focus is only achieved within a syntactical context of language. As the child develops a continually wider ability to create ever greater complexity of gestalten in play, thought, and word, the shape and meaning of his own perceptual world emerges, and the continual interplay of perceptual relations with environment sharpens the contours of his own image and deepens the reflections of the effects of his own identity on others.

EIGHT

Creative Evolution: A Process of Compassion

MANKIND is (and has been, since the emergence of *Homo sapiens*) biologically the same, and man has always felt this need to know and to organize the world around him, as, indeed, we now find is the case with many animals. The greatest variations in general behavior between early and contemporary cultures are of technological origin. From this standpoint, cultures tend to become more and more complex as technology is developed and creates more highly differentiated instruments, permitting more complex interpretations of nature as well as more complex interrelations among men.

These changes entail not only a continually deepening cosmic world image in terms of time and space, but also new languages that describe what men do, providing in turn more highly differentiated types of human behavior. Thus, man's story of his own nature is only half of the human story; the other half is man's evolving image of nature-as-cosmos.

Changing imagery in the language of natural description—following changing technology deriving from the advancement of science—inevitably brings about changes of pattern in man's relations with nature. Werner Heisenberg[95] has noted that

> when we speak of a picture of nature provided by contemporary exact science, we do not actually mean any longer a picture of nature, but rather a picture of our relation to nature. . . . Science no longer is in the position of observer of nature, but rather recognizes itself as part of the interplay between man and nature.[96]

The human metaphor (to use Elizabeth Sewell's[97] phrase) is not absent from this discussion, for Heisenberg further comments that natural science always presupposes man and we must become aware of the fact. As Bohr[98] has expressed it, we are not only spectators, but also participants on the stage of life, which John Dollard has felicitously described as the "theatre of perception." Physicist, social scientist, and poet employ similar metaphorical logic to describe man's functional need to achieve an exodus into the three- and four-dimensional continuum—a world image in which others share.

In keeping with the spirit of research in art and science in our present era, contemporary critical explorations in the arts seem to be aiming intuitively toward a vocabulary that will interpret the creative principles of art in terms of physics, in order to bring "Cosmos and History" (to quote a title of Mircea Eliade[99]) within the continuity of some dynamic forward-moving unitary principle.

When focusing attention upon childhood as the most specific biological peculiarity in human life history, we find ourselves at an intersection of biological and cultural evolution, with perspectives leading both into the past and toward the future.

We know a good deal about man's achievement of those discontinuities from animal impulse and instinct that have enabled him to create cultures but divided him from the rest of nature (from which he has nevertheless evolved and with which he remains united physiologically). We know very little about the creative effect on perception and mind of those rhythmical continuities, visual, auditory, tactile, or metabolic, that support the system of the body and unite its organs of research with systems in nature.

As the climax to a study of animal learning, William Thorpe presents us with some clues that lead these concepts into our subject of the early development of knowledge in man as child:

> Biological organisation now seems increasingly apparent in circumstances and conditions where not so long ago all was thought to be physics and chemistry, and it seems that further advances may come as a result of starting with concepts derived from biological systems and working back into the physical sciences.[100]

Thorpe's point is that in "working back" we are using a depth analysis of nature, which has permitted new syntheses of physics and chemistry within biological wholeness. In this case, surely we are not extrapolating too far in relating the principle of organization in nature's behavior directly to human imagination, the organizing behavior of mind that creates novelty in thought. The physics of the body and nature as universe remain the generating forces, but evolution, rather than growth, is the proper metaphor for the process of the developing mind.

Although structured language—that is, language with grammar and syntax—is indeed the greatest difference between animals and humans, the true scope of human cognitive processes continues to lie in plasticity of perception, by means of which mutual relations between systems in nature and systems of the body can be organized into form and meaning in linguistic or aesthetic form.

Animals, too, use symbols, and some species employ behavior that can be referred to as language (as is the case with bees), because this behavior communicates. But only man has used language as the basis of cultural and technological evolution by means of systems of symbols. Constructive cultural evolution, in my view, is an enrichment of human relations with environment that alters man's attitudes and sentiments toward the world and his fellow men.

For example, as early as the twelfth century the new current in Western thought that poetized woman and child in religious and literary observance coincided with a new perspective of nature in art. Erwin Panofsky has characterized this view as marking a period of belief in a "direct *intuitus* from subject to object"[101] in sensory experience. This is very much in keeping with the concepts of modern gestalt psychology. The senses were observed to be sources of information for the higher synthesizing work of mind; a new sequence of ideas of nature as reality was set in motion from which new attitudes toward the natural world were to emerge. These attitudes would in turn release wholly different narrative explanations of his own nature by man. A climate was forming that would eventually permit the concept of biological evolution, the most powerful long-term metaphor for history to emerge from the mind of man, to make its appearance as a tool of thought.

According to Julian Huxley, "Man is evolution become conscious." Speaking specifically of problems of our human future, Huxley writes, "Our new pattern of thinking will be evolution-centred. It will give us assurance by reminding us of our long evolutionary rise; how this was also, strangely and wonderfully, the rise of the mind. . . . Life is and must be a continuum because of its basic processes of self-reproduction: in the perspective of time, all living matter is continuous because every fresh portion of it has been produced by living things."[102] From the point of view developed in this work, there is an aesthetic diagrammatic logic in Huxley's overall mapping of natural history, which also accounts for the discontinuities that produce form and individuality.

"Discontinuities," Huxley states, "have been introduced into the continuum which are of first-rate significance to a long-term view of evolution." Living forms have boundaries even at the cellular level. But "in biological reality in all cases, the discontinuity although fundamental is never absolute." Because of "the limitation of the cell theory and the impossibility of giving a rigid definition of organic individuality . . . cells remain essential biological units . . . part of nature's continuum and yet separate. The same applies to species" (ibid.).

As man, woman, or child, we are living portions of the vast historical continuum that is nature. At the level of mind and culture, the problem of identity becomes both psychological and philosophical and turns toward relations between the individual and the multitude. At the level of individual personality, the problem of achieving a singular identity enters the realm of the psychology of medicine, which in turn is found to be a problem of biocultural adaptation to environment and to the worlds of one's fellow man.

Margaret Mead, following the pattern of centering on evolution, carries the argument forward into cultural continuities.[103] This study implies that human evolution is biocultural as well as psychocultural or psychosocial. The point is that the strength of cultural development is to be found in its continuities with biological roots, rather than in the equally essential but overstressed achievement of discontinuities from animal instinct and impulse —discontinuities that we know, to be essential, however, to the attainment of cultural transcendence of biological levels of behavior, in particular aggressive and sexual behavior.

If we put aside idealization of permanence or set goals and observe growth and learning in childhood as a period of gradual transcendence from level to level, out of biological nature into culturally created worlds, we become more conscious of the contributions, in the shape of values and even skills, which these earlier phases of personal history and biocultural development make to the fully adult personality. We then find ourselves in possession of the connection between biological history and cultural history, with individual childhood as the link in the series in time.

We tend to think more specifically of biological production of form from the standpoint of procreation. But biologically speaking, the growth of the individual is an activity of multicellular form production in itself, a striving toward self-fulfillment. This is the behavior pattern of our bodies as energy systems within evolution, the history that links us individually with all of nature's strivings toward variation and multiplicity of form.

Historical change, like personal change, is an adaptation of metaphoric relations to the environment, based on variations in the psychological pattern of human relations between man, woman, and child and between the individual and the multitude; such changes are often prefigured in verbal imagery and seized upon by the prefigurative imagination of creative, poetic minds. The emergence of the child as the key to creative relations with nature was prefigured in the philosophy of poets long before there was any understanding of the importance of childhood to the body–mind sequence of psychological health.

In their awareness of the creative significance of the child's perceptual worldmaking, Coleridge and Wordsworth, like Goethe and Blake, were far ahead of the twentieth-century psychiatric schools that have concentrated entirely on the role of childhood as it appears in psychopathology. By Wordsworth's and Coleridge's time the deepening imagery of reflection, brought about by the greater and more generalized opportunity for reading, combined with a far greater vocabulary of perception of nonpersonal worlds of nature. As C. S. Lewis describes the emergence of this "birth of a new world," a great turning inward was created when reading became a mode of perception. This inner reflectiveness was wonderfully depicted at its outset by St. Augustine, "the fields, the caves, the dens of Memory cannot be counted. . . . I force my way in amidst them, even as far as my power reaches, and nowhere find an end."[104] This journey inward had by the nineteenth century become a spiraling journey between inwardness and outwardness, between the two natures, human and natural, where poetry and science joined in words; the same vocabularies of perception began to "work" in both realms.

The comparison of the natural genius of the child with the cultivated inventiveness of adult genius, especially at the highest levels, is justified by the fact that both ages are in search of *true metaphor*—"true correspondences" in Erikson's wording, which release the organizing powers of mind and nervous system into action and the making of meaning.

Historically speaking, individual genius has played the principal role in the achievement of a general cultural transcendence of previous levels, both psychological and cultural, by introducing

higher forms of ability, purpose, and aim into the cultural continuum. The genius of childhood, in the sense of extreme originality
and the creation of personal worlds that induce mutations in cultural evolution, is discontinuous and persists into adult life only as
a specialized, highly cultivated condition (as in the case of Einstein).

> To carry on the feelings of childhood into the powers of manhood,
> to combine the child's sense of wonder and novelty with the
> appearance which every day for perhaps forty years has rendered
> familiar:
>> With sun and moon and stars throughout the year
>> And man and woman.
> This is the character and privilege of genius.   (Source unknown.)

The role of the exceptional individual in cultural evolution is
clear when we realize that religious interpretations of man in
nature have mobilized and directed entire cultures. We must recognize the role of the gifted individual, the prophet or seer, the
charismatic personality in religious movements. In such individu-
als the structure of personality as a hierarchical continuum; the
conscious responses of the ascending, evolving knowledge of his
own nervous system in childhood; the identification with biological figures; the participation in ecological levels of nature—all
will be incorporated in the structure of his beliefs and thus transferred to the cultures that adopt them.

In allowing these successive levels of human development a
rightful share in historical achievement, we can recognize its full
partnership in the long, slow evolution of culture. In the language
of science today the images of nature and the human body are so
closely conjoined that we are always near to the very roots of
emergent mind, although at differing levels of thought.

So it is to the world of childhood and learning in childhood that
we must turn. The philosophy of personality of today (as in
ancient Greece) is shaped in terms of medicine or medical psychology, but as the mystic poet Thomas Traherne recognized in
the seventeenth century, it is "taught in negatives," while the

"felicity" of learning to learn "remains a glorious though an unknown thing."[105]

If, as I assume, all cultural innovation derives from the impulse that produces play during the period of growth and fulfillment of biological form in childhood, then Thorpe's words about "true play"—an idea linked to Barfield's idea of "true metaphor" and Erikson's idea of "true correspondences"—can be placed within this context of cultural evolution. According to Thorpe,

> True play is to be expected where appetitive behaviour becomes emancipated from the restriction imposed by the necessity of attaining a specific goal. Such play can lead (and in evolution appears to have led in birds and mammals) to an enormous widening of perceptual horizons and thus to the development of exploratory drive. Thus the process of freeing appetitive behaviour from the primary needs increases perception of and mastery over the environment, and must have been one of the first and perhaps the most important of the behaviour changes which made possible the development of social life in the vertebrates, and indeed ultimately the mental and spiritual life of man himself.[106]

This remarkable insight seems to have been overlooked by many in search of man's future in cultural evolution. Yet it leads into those ideas about man and universe that are now coming into the foreground. Buckminster Fuller, who particularly and most profitably enjoys voyaging among the stars in the cosmos, states in a lecture, "Vision 65":

> There are many indications . . . that man is just about to begin to participate consciously and somewhat more knowingly and responsibly in his own evolutionary transformation. I include evolution of the environment as a major part of the evolution of humanity.

Despite our catastrophic errors such as war and destruction of the environment, Fuller continues, "if we discover that man is necessary to the invention of the universe, we can understand somewhat better what he is inadvertently doing."[107]

The understanding of play in childhood is an entering wedge into an epistemology that could release realization of the impulse toward self-transcendence as a survival function. Recognizing the child's worldmaking play as a biocultural continuity of evolutionary striving, we can examine questions about individual modes of transcendence. The study of learning can then move away from existentialist methods into areas that would appeal to natural selection in human societies.

According to Dubos, man is an animal linked to inanimate matter, but human life transcends its earthly origin. The question of what we mean by transcendence is central to the future development of man. In the past the term has been most closely associated with religious striving and achievement, but there is a marked similarity between motivation in religious striving toward higher levels and biological or evolutionary transcendence of organisms toward higher strata. This resemblance is so marked that a relatedness of meaning seems latent or implied in the use of the metaphor of transcendence in differing contexts.

In the living world, within either a religious context or the context of biological evolution, ideas of transcendence indicate an emergence from past time and space into present toward future and higher levels. A sense of futurity is implied or involved, as well as a rise in levels of organization. Man is a cosmic animal, with a primordial preoccupation with temporal and spatial relations and with the future in time.

Depth analysis of the mind's relations with environment has not ventured with sufficient profundity into experience of man's cosmic sense of time and space, although the experience is organismic and universal; it is also a primordial concern in childhood at organismic levels—with perceptual evolution as a learning process.

Transcendence cannot be finite. It would be folly for any individual to claim to know or define the nature of transcendence as either a biological or a cultural process. As ultimate end, bioculturally speaking, it is forever retreating from view. And certain it is that in human life, self-transcendence is not essentially intellectual. As many a religion has intuitively surmised, self-transcendence is a process in human compassion, a development of compassionate intelligence in which humility is the creative tool.

The development of compassionate intelligence as a cultural

goal is as yet a segregated technique, all too often only awakened into conscious, social action after disaster. Yet it has a neurophysiological basis in the impulse to nurture the child—an impulse that has certainly moved upward and forward into our social institutions that nurture, cultivate, or heal the human mind and body. We can, however, move back, far down evolutionary history, and find the animal instinct to nurture the young present in a vast number of species, while plant life also displays many examples of mutuality between plant and seedling "young," enclosing, covering, or protecting the coming generation. It is the pattern of action in evolutionary history that counts at this point —the pattern which has survived through natural selection and has finally been transmitted to mammals and ultimately to humans as a culturally and emotionally conditioned process.

Philosophically speaking, we have been faced with an unexplained void between man and nature, between cultural history and natural history; this void is in itself basically disturbing in a subliminal way, for we find ourselves historically placed in and a part of the animal kingdom without any explanation as to how we became human. Culture as the special invention of man, which in actuality bestows upon the individual the power to express evolutionary strivings and to transcend animal impulse in cultural form, is all too often seen as a sort of conjuring trick of the mind. Mind remains cut off from body in an implied, if not directly stated, dualism.

The twentieth-century concept of culture, a complex historical achievement by means of which man maintains his humanity, is a definition of human behavior that we owe to anthropology, above all to such cultural anthropologists as Franz Boas, Ruth Benedict, Bronislaw Malinowski, Margaret Mead, and all those true fieldworkers who went beyond abstractions in order to bring the full meaning of art and artifact, of pattern and form in behavior, into the forefront of exploration. In this context we now have access to the full measure and value of the triple theme of man–woman–child perceived as interwoven within the cognitive experience of every living being, forming also the basic biological experience out of which culture and personality have been conceived, evolved, and imaginatively expanded by the mind of man.

With our additional knowledge of the unused potential of the child, we are in a position to evaluate the power of this potential as the evolutionary striving. If, in addition, we take stock of our established awareness of the possibility of early psychic injury, we find ourselves facing once more the counterpoint between life and death—the life and death of a nascent soul and possibly of the human race. Recollection of creative perception and early learning in childhood can then be recognized as remembrance of the sense of evolutionary potential, which in childhood is actually a survival need—the need to know, learn, and organize. This awareness, which now functions only in latent form, presents man with a new theme to exploit in his historical development, both personal and cultural.

Compassionate intelligence permits the kind of understanding and sharing of "otherness" that we call "identification." To generalize this ability as a skill in learning would lead to a use of the humanities seldom encountered today. When generalizing about the possibility of applying methods of identification and compassionate insight to the understanding of motivation in mankind as a whole, we must recognize the destructiveness in ourselves as well as in others (which is essentially implied by the Socratic axiom "Know thyself"). At the same time, this knowledge needs to be matched by an awareness that at some time every human being experiences a profound longing to be good. This level of insight or truly compassionate intelligence requires an attitude of humility about knowledge as the first step. To "become as a child" is a far more subtle idea than is generally assumed. The drive and ability of the poet (and in a far simpler form, of the child) to become what he wishes to know or understand derives from a combination of wonder and a sense of "something far more deeply interfus'd," an acceptance of not knowing, which brings with it a special type of humility infused with joy.

The experience of sheer growth and training is for each child a matter of constant choice between good and ill as knowledge increases. Unfortunately it was all too often assumed by nine-teenth-century cultures with a history of puritanism that we must kill the animal in our own nature; in the twentieth century it has become clear that we must domesticate the animal in ourselves. This is only possible if we acknowledge not only the danger but also the value latent in animal drives and appetites. For self-tran-scendence is the result of both a spiritual and an ecological pat-tern of purposeful striving, the working of energy in individual human beings when they adapt to and create their own environ-ment in a manner conducive to communal life. A highly stylized contempt for the subjective as totally irrational permeates our everyday living, excluding the development of aesthetic interest at its historical source.

The twentieth-century attitude toward childhood has brought awareness of this major biocultural human phase to a state of ripe-ness that has forced us to reevaluate all our concepts of human behavior in terms of personal history. The journey into the depths of personality becomes a journey into biological history, produc-ing a complexity in modern consciousness that forces us to contin-ually reexamine the implication of "meaning" to an extent hereto-fore unknown in the history of thought. The very term "semantic" is a newcomer in the field of general knowledge, and this fact in itself is evidence of the uncertainty we feel about the relations between word and image.

Although we are biologically one with our preliterate ancestors, we are continually reaching new levels of insight into human nature at one end of the spectrum of mind, while at the other we are continually identifying a greater complexity and continuity of relations between mind and nature, to a point at which the hori-zons of human history recede into the background of the long evolution of animal forms that preceded the appearance of man.

This realignment of the relation between the meaning of experi-ence and culturally created information systems in terms of more contemporary knowledge is like the child's continual early experi-mentation with the links between perception and words during the process of creating his world image. And this process markedly resembles the method of the poet in creating the world of the poem. In these dynamic, plastic fields of thought, language is an instrument of exploration, not a tool for the exposition of facts.

We are now in a position to make much more fruitful use of this comparison between child and poet than ever before, but not in the form of the cult of the child, as has been the general trend, particularly since the eighteenth century, in both literary and social worlds of discourse. The comparison now serves as a valuable guide to progression in learning and to the development of the rich and whole personality within our evolving, dynamic world image, in which ecology as the science of mutual relations between organisms and their total environment now plays a leading role. In the creative perceptions of poet and child we are close to the biology of thought itself—close, in fact, to the ecology of imagination, in which the energies of the body and mind as a unit, an ecosystem, and the energies of nature combine in a mutual endeavor to adapt to nature, to culture, and to the societies devised by man to embody culture.

Yet the narrowing of the focus of research and exploration within the dimensions of the single individual as a body image is also cutting us out of the continuum in which we live and breathe. For, although the Socratic position "Know thyself" is unquestionably essential to the long, slow, and only half-realized awareness of the uniqueness of human individuality, this idea is now running rampant in the guise of self-improvement and a detachment from responsibility for anything that occurs beyond the private realm of self-realization. The iconography of man as individual has assumed the appearance of a figure in a collage perched on the surface of a jumbled picture of bread and circuses. Self-gratification as a way of life reigns supreme, often wearing the mask of cultural idealism. Many a young person succumbs to this directive with the best of intentions, only to find that the search comes to a dead end with a mirror image of selfhood and insatiable appetites.

Years of work with autobiographical recollections of childhood have made me wish to dispute vigorously the claim that learning to know oneself produces the kind of ego strength and culturally acceptable identity that the world so sorely needs. It is indeed only in the "to-and-fro" comparative metaphorical work of creating his image of the world and his fellow men that the individual achieves a true sense of identity and brings the image of selfhood into focus.

Body image and world image overlap in the work of the perceiving nervous system; the identity of each and every person is, therefore, an ego–world unity. But richness of personality in a culturally valuable sense can only be measured in terms of human relations and the capacity of the individual for compassionate intelligence. This intelligence has clearly evolved from the reciprocity of the mother–child relationship and has its roots far down the evolutionary tree, far below the level of human nature. The fruits of this intelligence are to be found in man's highest cultural and social institutions, such as medicine and education, which are in actuality highly evolved forms of nurture.

The individual moves in a world that is the direct outcome of personal interpretation, translated into culturally monitored language systems and systems of meaning. It is from this standpoint that we begin to see the extraordinary advantages as well as the great disadvantages that compose the human condition, and come to appreciate more sympathetically the dangers inherent in the biological specializations of the human body considered in relation to the levels we call "mind." Overspecialization, which creates rigidity of response, is a formidable threat to any species, occasionally resulting in extinction through sheer inability to change and adapt, as for instance with the gigantism of the dinosaurs.

The human specialization with which we are most familiar today is our prolonged postnatal infancy, a condition that has probably evoked the human need to extend learning behavior. We now understand something about the aftereffects of the lack of expression of sexual potential in childhood on psychological trends and patterns of behavior in adult life. However, overspecialization of interest to the point of pathology could drive man's cultural values into a downgrading process, which would lead to an adolescent fixation on selfhood.

Stifling of evolutionary striving could lead to extinction of the race through lack of interest in ecological or mutual relations between man and man and between man and nature. We do not as yet understand how to put to full use the strength of the child's appetitive need for the power to know and to create his environment, nor do we know how to fully exploit the depth of the human urge to continue to find satisfaction in knowledge of the outer world. Whereas sexual aims and purposes require moral restraints and restrictions in order to curb, narrow, and civilize sexual behavior, the striving to evolve richer and more creative relations with environment requires continual expansion of cultural aims and social purposes that act as releasers for the formative energy of this development. As in sexual behavior, unused energy of the body seeking to fulfill this psychological and mental trend will be displaced onto the ingenuity of delinquency and crime.

The common-plus-cosmic sense of the beginnings of the child's thought establishes a basic need for outer expression of the power to model and mold his environment. This can be achieved through cooperation and mutual relations with his total environment, in which learning, imagination, and the process of evolution will be geared to one another in the child's personal development. If cultural attitudes could be shifted toward a recognition of human desire to exercise a compassionate intelligence, not only as tool and method but also as the chief human survival function, we would, I believe, find ourselves capitalizing on the human impulse to nurture, cultivate, and extend this vast potential. It is even conceivable that the economic motive, which at present dominates social structure and stifles other styles of motivation, could be enlisted if all humanity's health and welfare were seen to be at stake. The counterpoint between life and death, even in wartime, tends to evoke man's nurturing impulses, thus developing new methods of healing that lead to new techniques of learning. When these conditions prevail, the world—or the particular ecological niche we inhabit—becomes in truth a "vale of soul-making," to quote Keats again. We are today in a position to release this creative drive in the world.

References

1. Gesell, Arnold. *The Embryology of Behavior.* New York: Harper, 1945.
2. Erikson, Erik. *Insight and Responsibility.* New York: Norton, 1964, p. 45.
3. Wordsworth, William. *The Prelude or the Growth of a Poet's Mind.* London: Oxford University Press, 1933.
4. Oppenheimer, J. Robert. *The Flying Trapeze: Three Crises for Physicists.* Oxford: Oxford University Press, 1964, p. 7.
5. Elton, Charles. *The Ecology of Animals,* 3rd ed. New York: Wiley, 1950 (first published in 1933).
6. Thorpe, William H. *Learning and Instinct in Animals,* 2nd rev. ed. Cambridge: Harvard University Press, 1963.
7. Deevey, Edward S., Jr. (1964). "General and Historical Ecology," *BioScience 14*:33–35.
8. Odum, Eugene (1964). "The New Ecology," *BioScience 14*:14–16.
9. Ibid., p. 16.
10. Modley, Rudolf. *How to Use Pictorial Statistics.* New York: Harper, 1937.
11. Koch, C. *The Tree Test: The Tree Drawing Test as an Aid in Psychodiagnosis.* Bern: Huber; New York: Grune and Stratton, 1952.
12. Buck, J. N. (1949). "The H–T–P Technique," *Journal of Clinical Psychology 5*:37–74.
13. Panofsky, Erwin. *Meaning in the Visual Arts.* Garden City, New York: Doubleday, 1955.
14. Klee, Paul. *The Thinking Eye* (transl. by Ralph Manheim). New York: Wittenborn, 1961.
15. Forman, Maurice Buxton (ed.). *The Letters of John Keats.* New York: Oxford, 1935.

16. Elton, *The Ecology of Animals*, 1950, p. 7.
17. Plato, *The Theaetetus* (155D).
18. Misch, Georg. *A History of Autobiography in Antiquity*. Cambridge: Harvard University Press, 1951.
19. Vico, Giambattista. *The Autobiography* (transl. by Max Harold Fisch and Thomas G. Bergin). Ithaca: Cornell University Press, 1944.
20. Untermeyer, Louis (ed.). *The Poetry and Prose of Walt Whitman*. New York: Simon and Schuster, 1949, pp. 346–48.
21. Berenson, Bernard. *Sketch for a Self-Portrait*. Toronto: Pantheon Books, 1949, p. 18.
22. Ibid., pp. 19–20.
23. Ibid., p. 20.
24. Ibid., p. 21.
25. Barfield, Owen. *Poetic Diction: A Study in Meaning*. London: Faber and Faber, 1952, p. 86 (first published in 1928).
26. Read, Herbert. Preface in L. L. Whyte (ed.), *Aspects of Form: A Symposium in Nature and Art*. London: Lund Humphries, 1951, p. v.
27. Klee, Paul, *The Thinking Eye*, 1961, pp. 81–82.
28. Freud, Sigmund. *The Standard Edition of the Complete Works of Sigmund Freud* (transl. by James Strachey, Anna Freud, et al.). London: Hogarth Press 1955. Vol. 18, p. 15.
29. Vaughan, Henry. "The Retreat." In F. Fogle (ed.), *The Complete Poetry of Henry Vaughan*. New York: Anchor Books, Doubleday, 1964, pp. 169–70.
30. Thorpe, *Learning and Instinct in Animals*, 1963.
31. Ibid., p. 9.
32. Ibid., p. 12.
33. Herrick, Charles Judson. *The Evolution of Human Nature*. Austin: University of Texas Press, 1956.
34. Gesell, *The Embryology of Behavior*, 1945, p. 46.
35. Ibid., pp. 61, 46.
36. Nabokov, Vladimir. *Speak, Memory: An Autobiography Revisited*. New York: Putnam, 1966, p. 300.
37. Ibid., p. 302.
38. Butterfield, H. *The Origins of Modern Science, 1300–1800*. New York: Macmillan, 1951.
39. Nabokov, *Speak, Memory*, 1966, p. 301.
40. Rorschach, Herman. *Psychodynamics*. Berne: Huber, 1942.
41. Gesell, *The Embryology of Behavior*, 1945, p. 106.
42. Polanyi, Michael. *Personal Knowledge; Towards a Post-Critical Philosophy*. New York: Harper and Row, 1964.
43. Elsasser, Walter M. *The Physical Foundation of Biology: An Analytical Study*. New York: Pergamon, 1958, p. 102.

44. Pollock, Thomas S. *The Nature of Literature.* Princeton: Princeton University Press, 1942, p. 22.
45. Thorpe, *Learning and Instinct in Animals,* 1963, p. 3.
46. Ibid., p. 104.
47. Polyani, *Personal Knowledge,* 1964, p. 80.
48. Korzybski, Alfred. *Science and Sanity,* 4th ed. Lakeville, Connecticut: International Non-Aristotelian Publishing Company, 1958.
49. Lowenfeld, Victor and Brittain, W. Lambert. *Creative and Mental Growth.* New York: Macmillan, 1964 (first published in 1947).
50. Cobb, Stanley. *Foundations of Neuropsychiatry,* 6th rev. ed. Baltimore: Williams & Wilkins, 1958, p. 83.
51. Ruyer, Raymond (1957). "The Vital Domain of Animals and the Religious World of Man," *Diogenes* Summer: 35–46.
52. Ibid., pp. 43–44.
53. Dollard, John. *Criteria for the Life History.* New Haven: Yale University Press, 1935.
54. Wiener, Norbert. *Cybernetics.* New York: Wiley, 1948.
55. Keller, Helen Adams. *The Story of My Life.* Garden City, New York: Doubleday, 1955.
56. Portmann, Adolf. *New Paths in Biology.* New York: Harper and Row, 1964.
57. Aiken, Conrad. *A Letter from Lipo and Other Poems.* New York: Oxford University Press, 1955, p. 27.
58. Ibid., p. 13.
59. Ibid., p. 18.
60. Wordsworth, *The Prelude,* 1933.
61. Fuller, R. Buckminster. 1966. "Vision 65" (summary lecture), *American Scholar* 35:206–18.
62. Berenson, Bernard. *Aesthetics and History in the Visual Arts.* New York: Pantheon, 1948, p. 72.
63. Ibid., p. 38.
64. Thompson, Sir D'Arcy Wentworth. *On Growth and Form,* 2nd ed. Cambridge: At the University Press, 1963, pp. 16, 10.
65. Ibid., p. 10.
66. Ibid., pp. 11, 10.
67. Ibid., p. 16.
68. Herrick, *The Evolution of Human Nature,* 1956, p. 292.
69. Dubos, René. *Man Adapting.* New Haven: Yale University Press, 1965, p. 42.
70. Ibid., p. 7.
71. Ibid., p. 22.
72. The story of Alice refers to a case presented at a staff conference during a hospital placement during Edith Cobb's social-work training.

73. Dubos, *Man Adapting*, 1965, p. xviii.
74. Ibid.
75. Ibid., p. 23.
76. Mill, John Stuart. *Autobiography of John Stuart Mill*. New York: Columbia University Press, 1960.
77. Ibid., p. 86.
78. Ibid., p. 83.
79. Coghill, G. E. *Anatomy and the Problem of Behavior*. London: Cambridge University Press, 1929.
80. Ratchford, Fannie E. *The Brontës' Web of Childhood*. New York: Russell/Atheneum, 1964 (first published in 1941).
81. Singer, Dorothea. *Giordano Bruno, His Life and Thought*. With annotated translation of his work, *On the Infinite Universe and Worlds*. New York: Schuman, 1950.
82. Brewster, Sir David. *Memoirs of the Life, Writings and Discoveries of Sir Isaac Newton*, 2 vols. New York: Johnston Reprint Corp., 1965, p. 407 (first published in 1855).
83. Needham, Joseph. *Science and Civilization in China*, vol. 2. Cambridge, England: University Press, 1956, p. 94.
84. Corte, Nicholas [pseud. L. Cristiani]. *Pierre Teilhard de Chardin, His Life and Spirit* (transl. by Martin Jarrett-Kerr). New York: Macmillan, 1960, p. 4.
85. Ibid.
86. Richards, Ivor A. *Mencius on the Mind: Experiments in Multiple Definition*. London: Paul, Trench, Trubner, 1932.
87. Sherrington, Sir Charles. *Man on His Nature*. Cambridge: At the University Press, 1946, p. 104.
88. Lorenz, Konrad. "The Role of Gestalt Perception in Animal and Human Behavior." In L. L. Whyte, (ed.), *Aspects of Form*. London: Lund Humphries, 1951, pp. 157–78; quotation, p. 176.
89. Deevey, "General and Historical Ecology," 1964, p. 3.
90. Clark, Sir Kenneth McKenzie. *Moments of Vision*. Oxford: Clarendon, 1954.
91. Ibid., p. 3.
92. Ibid., p. 4.
93. Pasternak, Boris. *I Remember* (transl. by David Magarshak). New York: Pantheon, 1959, p. 15.
94. Wordsworth, *The Prelude*, 1933, p. 27.
95. Heisenberg, Werner (1958). "The Representation of Nature in Contemporary Physics," *Daedalus* Summer: 95–108.
96. Ibid., p. 107.
97. Sewell, Elizabeth. *The Human Metaphor*. Notre Dame, Indiana: University of Notre Dame Press, 1964.

98. Quoted by Heisenberg, "The Representation of Nature in Contemporary Physics," 1958.
99. Eliade, Mircea. *Cosmos and History: The Myth of the Eternal Return* (transl. by William R. Trask). New York: Pantheon, 1954.
100. Thorpe, *Learning and Instinct in Animals*, 1963, p. 415.
101. Panofsky, *Meaning in the Visual Arts*, 1955, p. 16.
102. Huxley, Julian S. *Essays of a Humanist*. New York: Harper and Row, 1964, p. 83.
103. Mead, Margaret. *Continuities in Cultural Evolution*. New Haven: Yale University Press, 1964.
104. Lewis, C. S. *The Allegory of Love*. London: Oxford University Press, 1953, p. 65 (first published in 1936).
105. Traherne, Thomas. *Centuries of Meditations*. London: P. J. and A. E. Dobell, 1927, p. 193.
106. Thorpe, *Learning and Instinct in Animals*, 1963, p. 99.
107. Fuller, "Vision 65," 1966, p. 212.

Biographies and Autobiographies of Childhood in Many Countries in The Edith McKeever Cobb Collection, Teachers College Library Columbia University

THIS UNIQUE bibliography of works collected over half a century will be a continuing source for research on the significance of culturally patterned childhood experience in the forms assumed by imagination in different countries and eras. It is a selection from the original collection presented to the New York School of Social Work in the mid 1950s and later transferred as a contribution to the Early Childhood Education Library at Teachers College of Columbia University. Edith Cobb subsequently made further gifts to the Teachers College Library. An autobiography is indicated by an asterisk and a biography by a double asterisk; countries have been indicated and the birth and death dates of authors given when they were known; references without asterisks are books on childhood experiences.

M. M.

*Abbott, Eleanor Hallowell, 1872–   . *Being Little in Cambridge When Everyone Else Was Big.* New York: Appleton-Century, 1936, 280 pp. (U.S.A.).

*Abrahams, Peter, 1919– . *Tell Freedom: Memories of Africa.* New York: Knopf, 1954, 370 pp. (South Africa).

*Acland, Eleanor Margaret (Cropper), d. 1933. *Good-Bye for the Present: The Story of Two Childhoods, Milly: 1878–88 and Ellen: 1913–24.* New York: Macmillan, 1935, 318 pp. (England).

**Adams, W. H. Davenport. *Childlife and Girlhood of Remarkable Women: A Series of Chapters from Female Biography.* London: Sonnenschein, 1883, 350 pp. (England).

*Agee, James, 1900–1955. *The Morning Watch.* Boston: Houghton-Mifflin, 1951, 120 pp. (U.S.A.).

*Aksakov, Sergyi Timofyevich, 1791–1859. *A Russian Schoolboy.* London: Oxford University Press, 1924, 288 pp. (Russia).

*——. *Years of Childhood.* London: Oxford University Press, 1923, 446 pp. (Russia).

*Aleichem, Sholom, 1859–1916. *The Great Fair: Scenes from My Childhood.* New York: Noonday Press, 1955, 306 pp. (Russia).

*Allinson, Francesca. *A Childhood.* London: Hogarth Press, 1937, 187 pp. (England).

*Armstrong, Martin Donisthorpe, 1882–1970. *Victorian Peep-Show.* London: Joseph, 1938, 158 pp. (England).

*Asquith, Cynthia Mary Evelyn (Charteris), 1887–1960. *Haply I May Remember.* London: Barrie, 1950, 237 pp. (England).

*Augustinus, Aurelius, 345–430. *The Confessions of Saint Augustine.* New York: Modern Library, 1949, 338 pp. (Carthaginian–Roman Empire).

*Baillie, Eileen. *The Shabby Paradise: The Autobiography of a Decade.* New York: British Book Center, 1959, 223 pp. (England).

*Baines, Frank, 1915– . *Look Towards the Sea.* London: Eyre and Spottiswoode, 1958, 255 pp. (England).

*Baring, Maurice, 1874–1945. *The Puppet Show of Memory.* London: Heinemann, 1922, 457 pp. (England).

*Barke, James, 1905–1958. *The Green Hills Far Away: A Chapter in Autobiography.* London: Collins, 1940, 288 pp. (Scotland).

*Barlow, Nora. *The Autobiography of Charles Darwin, 1809–1882. With Original Omissions Restored.* London: Collins, 1958, 253 pp. (England).

Barrie, James Matthew. *The Little White Bird*. London: Hedder and Stoughton, 1902, 312 pp. (England).

*Baynes, Dorothy Julia (Dormer Creston). *Enter a Child*. London: Macmillan, 1939, 231 pp. (England).

**——. *The Youthful Queen Victoria: A Discursive Narrative*. London: Macmillan, 1952, 484 pp. (England).

*Beauvoir, Simone de, 1908– . *Memoirs of a Dutiful Daughter*. Cleveland: World, 1959, 382 pp. (France).

*Bell, Adrian, 1901– . *The Balcony*. New York: Simon and Schuster, 1935, 248 pp. (England).

*Berenson, Bernhard, 1865–1959. *Sketch for a Self-Portrait*. New York: Pantheon, 1949, 184 pp. (Lithuania; U.S.A.).

*Berners, Gerald Hugh Tyrwhitt-Wilson, 1883–1950. *A Distant Prospect*. London: Constable, 1945, 125 pp. (England).

*——. *First Childhood*. New York: Farrar and Rinehart, 1934, 273 pp. (England).

*Betjeman, John, 1906– . *Summoned By Bells*. Boston: Houghton-Mifflin, 1960, 97 pp. (England).

*Bjarnhof, Karl, 1898–   . *The Stars Grow Pale*. New York: Knopf, 1958, 310 pp. (Denmark).

*Borland, Hal, 1900– . *High, Wide and Lonesome*. Philadelphia: Lippincott, 1956, 251 pp. (U.S.A.).

*Bottome, Phyllis, 1884–1963. *Search for a Soul*. New York: Reynal and Hitchcock, 1948, 306 pp. (England).

*Bowen, Elizabeth, 1899– . *Seven Winters: Memories of a Dublin Childhood*. London: Longmans, Green, 1943, 48 pp. (Ireland).

Boyer, Francois. *The Secret Game*. New York: Harcourt, Brace, 1950, 187 pp. (France).

*Brant, Alice (Dayrell). *The Diary of "Helena Morley."* New York: Farrar, Straus and Cudahy, 1957, 281 pp. (Brazil).

*Bridge, Ann (pseud.), 1889–1939, see O'Malley, Mary Dolling.

*Bridie, James, 1888–1951. *One Way of Living*. London: Constable, 1939, 299 pp. (Scotland).

*Brooks, Jocelyn. *The Dog at Clambercrown: An Excursion*. London: Bodley Head, 1955, 256 pp. (England).

*Brown, Christy, 1932– . *My Left Foot*. London: Secker and Warburg, 1954, 192 pp. (Ireland).

Brown, John Mason. *Morning Faces: A Book of Children and Parents*. London: Hamish Hamilton, 1950, 187 pp. (U.S.A.).

*Buchan, John (Lord Tweedsmuir), 1875–1940. *Pilgrim's Way: An Essay in Recollection.* Boston: Houghton-Mifflin, 1940, 336 pp. (England).

*Burke, Norah, 1907– . *Jungle Child.* New York: Norton, 1956, 278 pp. (India).

*Burke, Thomas, 1887–1945. *Son of London.* London: Jenkins, 1946, 223 pp. (England).

*Burlingame, Roger, 1889–1967. *I Have Known Many Worlds.* Garden City, New York: Doubleday, 1959, 283 pp. (U.S.A.).

*Butts, Mary, 1892–1937. *The Crystal Cabinet: My Childhood at Salterns.* London: Methuen, 1937, 279 pp. (England).

*Byrne, Muriel St. Clare, 1895–1974. *Common or Garden Child: A Not Unfaithful Record.* London: Faber and Faber, 1942, 187 pp. (England).

*Canton, William, 1845–1926. *The Invisible Playmate: W. V., Her Book and In Memory of W. V.* New York: Dutton, 1912, 233 pp. (England).

**Carbery, Mary (Toulmin), 1867–1949. *The Farm by Lough Gur: The Story of Mary Fogarty (Sissy O'Brien).* London: Longmans, Green, 1937, 282 pp. (Ireland).

*——. *Happy World: The Story of a Victorian Childhood.* London: Longmans, Green, 1941, 273 pp. (Ireland).

*Cardus, Neville, 1899– . *Autobiography.* London: Collins, 1947, 288 pp. (England).

Cary, Joyce, 1888–1957. *Charley is My Darling.* London: Joseph, 1940, 413 pp. (Ireland).

*——. *A House of Children.* London: Joseph, 1951, 239 pp. (Ireland).

*Chagall, Bella (Rosenfeld), 1895–1944. *Burning Lights.* New York: Schocken, 1946, 268 pp. (Russia).

*Chagall, Marc, 1887– . *Ma Vie.* Dijon, France: Darantiere, 1957, 250 pp. (Russia).

*Chamson, Andre, 1900– . *A Time to Keep.* London: Faber and Faber, 1957, 315 pp. (France).

*Chiang, Lee, 1903– . *A Chinese Childhood.* New York: Day, 1952, 303 pp. (China).

*Chotzinoff, Samuel, 1889–1964. *A Lost Paradise: Early Reminiscences.* New York: Knopf, 1955, 373 pp. (U.S.A.).

*Church, Richard, 1893–1972. *The Golden Sovereign.* New York: Dutton, 1957, 245 pp. (England).

*——. *Over the Bridge: An Essay in Autobiography.* London: Heinemann, 1955, 231 pp. (England).

*Codrington, Kenneth de Burgh. *Cricket in the Grass.* London: Faber and Faber, 1959, 240 pp. (England).

*Colette, Sidonie Gabrielle, 1873–1954. *My Mother's House and Sido.* New York: Farrar, Straus, and Young, 1953, 219 pp. (France).

*Collier, Richard, 1924– . *A House Called Memory.* London: Collins, 1960, 189 pp. (England).

*Collingwood, R. G., 1889–1943. *An Autobiography.* London: Oxford University Press, 1939, 167 pp. (England).

*Colum, Padraic, 1881–1972. *The Flying Swans.* New York: Crown, 1957, 538 pp. (Ireland; U.S.A.).

*Cooper, Diana (Manners), 1892–   . *The Rainbow Comes and Goes.* Boston: Houghton-Mifflin, 1958, 271 pp. (England).

*Coyle, Kathleen, 1886–1952. *The Magical Realm.* New York: Dutton, 1943, 314 pp. (Ireland).

*Cropton, John. *The Road to Nowhere.* London: Hurst and Blackett, 1936, 288 pp. (England).

*Daiches, David, 1912– . *Two Worlds: An Edinburgh Jewish Childhood.* New York: Harcourt, Brace, 1956, 192 pp. (Scotland).

Davis, Clyde Brion (ed). *Eyes of Boyhood.* Philadelphia: Lippincott, 1953, 323 pp. (U.S.A.).

*Day-Lewis, Cecil, 1904–72. *The Buried Day.* New York: Harper, 1960, 243 pp. (Ireland).

De La Mare, Walter. *Memoirs of a Midget.* London: Collins, 1921, 365 pp. (England).

*Deland, Margaret Wade (Campbell), 1857–1945. *If This Be I, As I Suppose It Be.* New York: Appleton-Century, 1935, 227 pp. (U.S.A.).

De La Roche, Mazo. *Beside a Norman Tower.* Boston: Little, Brown, 1934, 247 pp. (England).

Del Castillo, Michel, 1933   . *Child of Our Time.* New York: Knopf, 1958, 281 pp. (Spain).

*Dennis, Geoffrey, 1892–1963. *Till Seven.* London: Eyre and Spottiswoode, 1957, 209 pp. (England).

*Dermoût, Mari, 1888–1962. *Yesterday: A Novel.* New York: Simon and Schuster, 1959, 118 pp. (Java).

*De Valois, Ninette, 1898–   . *Come Dance With Me: A Memoir, 1898–1956.* Cleveland: World, 1957, 254 pp. (Ireland).

*Dewes, Simon. *A Suffolk Childhood*. London: Hutchinson, 1959, 214 pp. (England).

Diamant, Gertrude. *The Days of Ofelia*. Boston: Houghton-Mifflin, 1942, 226 pp. (Mexico).

*Dickson, Horatio Lovat, 1902–   . *The Ante-Room*. London: Macmillan, 1959, 270 pp. (Australia).

*Djilas, Milovan, 1911–   . *Land Without Justice*. New York: Harcourt, Brace, 1958, 365 pp. (Yugoslavia).

*Dreiser, Theodore, 1871–1945. *Dawn*. New York: Liveright, 1931, 589 pp. (U.S.A.).

Duffus, Robert Luther. *Williamstown Branch: Impersonal Memories of a Vermont Boyhood*. New York: Norton, 1958, 252 pp. (U.S.A.).

*Du Maurier, George Louis Palmella Busson, 1834–1896. *Peter Ibbetson*. New York: Harper, 1891, 418 pp. (France).

Dunsany, Edward John Moreton Drax Plunkett. *Rory and Bran*. New York: Putnam, 1937, 320 pp. (Ireland).

*Durrell, Gerald Malcolm, 1925–   . *My Family and Other Animals*. London: Hart-Davis, 1956, 255 pp. (England; Greece).

Fane, Julian. *Morning*. New York: Reynal, 1957, 207 pp. (England).

*Farjeon, Eleanor, 1881–1965. *Portrait of a Family with Many Illustrations*. New York: Frederick Stokes, 1936, 456 pp. (England).

*Ferguson, Rachel. *We Were Amused: Memoirs*. London: Jonathan Cape, 1958, 258 pp. (England).

*Fisher, Douglas. *Little World*. London: Sylvan, 1948, 198 pp. (England).

*Fisher, Herbert Albert Laurens, 1865–1940. *An Unfinished Autobiography*. London: Oxford University Press, 1940, 163 pp. (England).

Fitzpatrick, Kathleen. *They Lived in County Down*. London: Chatto and Windus, 1937, 240 pp. (Ireland).

Flavin, Martin. *The Enchanted*. New York: Harper, 1947, 289 pp. (England).

*Fletcher, Peter, 1896–   . *The Long Sunday*. London: Faber and Faber, 1958, 188 pp. (England).

*Flexner, Helen Thomas. *A Quaker Childhood*. New Haven: Yale University Press, 1940, 335 pp. (U.S.A.).

*Fournier, Alain, 1886–1914. *The Wanderer*. Boston: Houghton-Mifflin, 1928, 306 pp. (France).

*Francis, Robert (Jean Godmé), 1901–   . *The Wolf at the Door*. Boston: Houghton-Mifflin, 1935, 470 pp. (France).

*Gary, Romain, 1914– . *Promise at Dawn.* New York: Harper, 1961, 337 pp. (Poland).

*Gide, André Paul Guillaume, 1869–1951. *If It Die.* London: Secker and Warburg, 1950, 301 pp. (France).

*Gill, Eric, 1882–1940. *Autobiography.* London: Jonathan Cape, 1940, 283 pp. (England).

*Girling, Zoe (pseud. Martin Hare). *Polonaise.* New York: Macmillan, 1940, 273 pp. (Poland).

*Giscard, John. *A Place of Stones.* London: Heinemann, 1958, 248 pp. (England).

*Glynne-Jones, William, 1907– . *The Childhood Land.* London: Batsford, 1960, 157 pp. (Wales).

*Goethe, Johann Wolfgang von, 1749–1832. *Goethe's Autobiography: Poetry and Truth from My Own Life.* Washington: Public Affairs Press, 1949, 700 pp. (Germany).

*Gorkii, Maksim, 1868–1936. *Childhood.* Moscow: Foreign Languages Publishing House, 1950, 442 pp. (Russia).

*Gosse, Edmund, 1849–1928. *Father and Son: Biographical Recollections.* New York: Scribners, 1908, 355 pp. (England).

Goudge, Elizabeth. *A City of Bells.* New York: Coward-McCann, 1936, 380 pp. (England).

——. *Island Magic.* New York: Coward-McCann, 1936, 352 pp. (England).

*Grahame, Kenneth, 1859–1932. *Dream Days.* London: John Lane, 1902, 227 pp. (England).

——. *First Whisper of "The Wind in the Willows."* London: Methuen, 1944, 89 pp. (England).

*——. *The Golden Age.* London: Nelson, 1908, 287 pp. (England).

Graham, Stephen. *Balkan Monastery: A Novel.* New York: Stokes, 1936, 328 pp. (Serbia).

*Grant, Joan (Marshall), 1907– . *Time Out of Mind.* London: Barker, 1956, 253 pp. (England).

*Green, Henry, 1905– . *Pack My Bag: A Self-Portrait.* London: Hogarth Press, 1940, 246 pp. (England).

*Green, Julien, 1900– . *Memories of Happy Days.* London: Dent, 1944, 216 pp. (France).

*Grierson, Francis, 1848–1927. *The Valley of Shadows.* Boston: Houghton-Mifflin, 1948, 278 pp. (U.S.A.).

*Griffith, Llewelyn Wyn, 1890– . *Spring of Youth.* New York: Dutton, 1935, 134 pp. (Wales).

*Griffith, Thomas, 1915– . *The Waist-High Culture.* New York: Harper, 1959, 275 pp. (U.S.A.).

*Hale, Edward Everett, 1822–1909. *A New England Boyhood and Other Bits of Autobiography.* Boston: Little, Brown, 1893, 267 pp. (U.S.A.).

*Hale, Nancy, 1908– . *A New England Girlhood.* Boston: Little, Brown, 1958, 232 pp. (U.S.A.).

*Hamilton, Iain, 1920– . *Half a Highlander: An Autobiography of a Scottish Youth.* New York: Dutton, 1957, 197 pp. (Scotland).

*Hamilton, Mary (Garnett), 1872– . *Green and Gold.* London: Wingate, 1948, 271 pp. (Ireland).

*Hannum, Alberta (Pierson), 1906– . *Spin a Silver Dollar: The Story of a Desert Trading-Post.* New York: Viking, 1945, 173 pp. (U.S.A.).

*Harding, Bertita (Leonarz), 1902– . *Mosaic in the Fountain.* Philadelphia: Lippincott, 1949, 320 pp. (Mexico).

*Harvey, William Fryer, 1885– . *We Were Seven.* London: Constable, 1936, 240 pp. (England).

*Hatsumi, Reiko. *Rain and the Feast of the Stars.* Boston: Houghton-Mifflin, 1959, 215 pp. (Japan).

*Hawker, Beatrice, 1910– . *Look Back in Love.* London: Longmans, Green, 1958, 149 pp. (England).

*Henrey, Robert, Mrs., 1906– . *The Little Madeleine.* New York: Dutton, 1953, 350 pp. (France).

*Heuss, Theodor, 1884–1963. *Preludes to Life: Early Memoirs.* London: Deutsch, 1955, 183 pp. (Germany).

*Hitchman, Janet, 1916– . *The King of the Barbareens: The Autobiography of an Orphan.* London: Putnam, 1960, 254 pp. (England).

*Holland, Vyvyan, 1887–1967. *Son of Oscar Wilde.* London: Hart-Davis, 1954, 272 pp. (England; Germany; Italy).

*Holman-Hunt, Diana. *My Grandmothers and I.* New York: Norton, 1960, 208 pp. (England).

*Horner, David. *Was It Yesterday?* London: Macmillan, 1939, 265 pp. (England).

*Howe, Bea. *Child in Chile.* London: Deutsch, 1957, 191 pp. (Chile).

*Hudson, William Henry, 1841–1922. *Far Away and Long Ago: A History of My Early Life.* New York: Dutton, 1918, 332 pp. (Argentina).

*Hughes, Mary Vivian (Thomas), 1866–   . *A London Child of the Seventies*. London: Oxford University Press, 1934, 173 pp. (England).

Hughes, Richard Arthur Warren. *The Innocent Voyage*. New York: Harper, 1929, 399 pp. (England).

*Huxley, Elspeth, 1907– . *The Flame Trees of Thika: Memories of an African Childhood*. London: Chatto and Windus, 1959, 288 pp. (Africa).

*Huxley, Julian Sorell, 1887–1975. *Religion Without Revelation*. New York: Harper, 1957, 252 pp. (England).

*Jackson, Annabel (Grant Duff), 1870–   . *A Victorian Childhood*. London: Methuen, 1932, 197 pp. (England).

*James, Henry, 1843–1916. *A Small Boy and Others*. London: Macmillan, 1913, 436 pp. (U.S.A.).

Jeffries, Richard. *Bevis: The Story of a Boy*. London: Duckworth, 1934, 464 pp. (England).

*Jones, Lawrence Evelyn, 1885–1969. *A Victorian Boyhood*. New York: St. Martin's, 1955, 244 pp. (England).

*Jones, Rufus Matthew, 1863–1948. *A Small-Town Boy*. New York: Macmillan, 1941, 154 pp. (U.S.A.).

*Joyce, James, 1882–1941. *A Portrait of the Artist as a Young Man*. New York: Modern Library, 1928, 299 pp. (Ireland).

Kassil, Leo. *The Land of Shvambrania*. New York: Viking, 1935, 289 pp. (Russia).

*Kästner, Erich, 1899–   . *When I Was a Little Boy*. London: Jonathan Cape, 1959, 187 pp. (Germany).

Kaye-Smith, Sheila. *Summer Holiday*. New York: Harper, 1932, 293 pp. (England).

*Kazin, Alfred, 1915– . *A Walker in the City*. New York: Harcourt, Brace, 1951, 176 pp. (U.S.A.).

*Keller, Helen Adams, 1880–1968. *The Story of My Life*. Garden City, New York: Doubleday, 1954, 382 pp. (U.S.A.).

*Kelly, Marie Noële. *Dawn to Dusk*. London: Hutchinson, 1960, 248 pp. (Belgium).

*Kendon, Frank. *The Small Years*. Cambridge: Cambridge University Press, 1930, 196 pp. (England).

*Kenward, James, 1908–   . *The Suburban Child*. Cambridge: Cambridge University Press, 1955, 141 pp. (U.S.A.).

*Kenyon, Katharine Mary Rose, 1887–   . *A House That Was Love*. London: Methuen, 1941, 253 pp. (England).

*Kipling, Rudyard, 1865–1936. *The Brushwood Boy*. New York: Doubleday, 1907, 73 pp. (England).

*——. *They*. New York: Doubleday, 1906, 80 pp. (England).

*Kirkup, James, 1918–1962. *The Only Child: An Autobiography of Infancy*. London: Collins, 1957, 191 pp. (England).

*Koizumi, Kazuo, 1893–   . *Father and I: Memories of Lafcadio Hearn*. Boston: Houghton-Mifflin, 1935, 208 pp. (Japan).

La Farge, Oliver. *Behind the Mountains*. Boston: Houghton-Mifflin, 1956, 179 pp. (U.S.A.).

*Lagerlöf, Selma Ottiliana Lovisa, 1858–1940. *Memories Of My Childhood: Further Years at Marbacka*. Garden City, New York: Doubleday, 1934, 290 pp. (Sweden).

*Laye, Camara, 1928–   . *The Dark Child*. New York: Noonday, 1954, 188 pp. (French Guinea).

*Lee, Laurie, 1914–   . *The Edge of Day: A Boyhood in the West of England*. New York: Morrow, 1960, 275 pp. (England).

Lee, Vernon. *The Child in the Vatican*. Portland, Maine: Thomas Mosher, 1910, 63 pp.

Lehmann, Rosamond. *The Ballad and the Source*. New York: Pocket Books, 1945, 343 pp. (England).

*Lewis, Clive Staples, 1898–1964. *Surprised by Joy: The Shape of My Early Life*. London: Bles, 1955, 224 pp. (England).

Lewis, Edith Nicholl. *As Youth Sees It: Personal Recollections of Great Victorians*. Boston: Meador, 1935, 187 pp. (England).

Lewis, Eiluned. *Dew on the Grass*. New York: Macmillan, 1934, 222 pp. (Wales).

*Lewis, Flannery. *Brooks Too Broad for Leaping: A Chronicle from Childhood*. New York: Macmillan, 1938, 274 pp. (U.S.A.).

Liddell, Robert. *Take This Child*. New York: Greystone Press, 1939, 347 pp. (England).

Lochhead, Marion. *Their First Ten Years: Victorian Childhood*. London: Murray, 1956, 247 pp. (England).

*Lord, Eda. *Childsplay*. New York: Simon and Schuster, 1961, 180 pp. (U.S.A.).

*Loti, Pierre (Julien Viaud), 1850–1923. *The Story of a Child*. Boston: Birchard, 1901, 304 pp. (France).

*Lowndes, Bessie Belloc, 1868–1947. *I Too Have Lived in Arcadia: A Record of Love and of Childhood*. London: Macmillan, 1941, 390 pp. (France).

*Lubbock, Percy, 1879–1965. *Earlham.* London: Jonathan Cape, 1922, 254 pp. (England).

*——. *Shades of Eton.* London: Jonathan Cape, 1929, 224 pp. (England).

*Lubbock, Sybil Marjorie (Cuffe), 1879–1943. *The Child in the Crystal.* London: Jonathan Cape, 1939, 318 pp. (England).

*Lutyens, Mary, 1908– . *To Be Young: Some Chapters of Autobiography.* London: Hart-Davis, 1959, 192 pp. (England).

*Lynch, Hannah, d. 1904. *Autobiography of a Child.* New York: Dodd, Mead, 1899, 270 pp. (U.S.A.).

*Lynch, Patricia, 1898– . *A Storyteller's Childhood.* London: Dent, 1947, 343 pp. (Ireland).

*MacCarthy, Mary Warre. *A Nineteenth-Century Childhood.* London: Secker, 1931, 159 pp. (England).

*Machen, Arthur, 1863–1947. *The Autobiography of Arthur Machen.* London: Richard, 1951, 308 pp. (England).

Mackenzie, Compton. *Sinister Street.* London: Bell, 1914, 496 pp. (England).

*Maclaren-Ross, Julian. *The Weeping and the Laughter: A Chapter of Autobiography.* London: Hart-Davis, 1953, 228 pp. (England).

*McCarthy, Mary Therese, 1912– . *Memories of a Catholic Girlhood.* New York: Harcourt, Brace, 1957, 245 pp. (U.S.A.).

*McHugh, Mary Frances. *Thalassa: A Story of Childhood by the Western Wave.* London: Macmillan, 1931, 217 pp. (Ireland).

*Malmberg, Bertil, 1889– . *Åke and His World.* New York: Farrar and Rinehart, 1940, 176 pp. (Sweden).

*Mankowitz, Wolf, 1924– . *A Kid for Two Farthings.* New York: Dutton, 1954, 120 pp. (England).

Mann, Thomas, 1875–1955. *Early Sorrow and Mario and the Magician.* London: Secker, 1934, 216 pp. (Germany).

*Masefield, John, 1878–1967. *So Long to Learn: Chapters of an Autobiography.* London: Heinemann, 1952, 242 pp. (England).

*Matthews, Thomas Stanley, 1901– . *Name and Address: An Autobiography.* New York: Simon and Schuster, 1960, 309 pp. (U.S.A.).

Maxwell, William. *The Folded Leaf.* New York: Vintage, 1959, 274 pp. (U.S.A.).

*May, James Lewis, 1873– . *The Path Through the Wood.* London: Bles, 1930, 195 pp. (England).

*——. *Thorn and Flower.* London: Bles, 1935, 249 pp. (England).

*Meyerstein, Edward Harry William, 1889–1952. *Of My Early Life: 1889–1918*. London: Spearman, 1957, 127 pp. (England).

Michaëlis, Karin. *Andrea: The Tribulations of a Child*. New York: McClure, Phillips, 1904, 141 pp. (Denmark).

*Mill, Anna Jean (ed.). *John Mill's Boyhood Visit to France: Being a Journal and Notebook Written by John Stuart Mill in France, 1820–21*. Toronto: University of Toronto Press, 1960, 133 pp. (England; France).

*Mill, John Stuart, 1806–1873. *Autobiography of John Stuart Mill*. New York: Columbia University Press, 1924, 240 pp. (England).

*Miller, Loye Holmes, 1874–   . *Lifelong Boyhood: Recollections of a Naturalist Afield*. Berkeley: University of California Press, 1950, 226 pp. (U.S.A.).

*Moberg, Vilhelm, 1898–   . *When I Was a Child*. New York: Knopf, 1956, 280 pp. (Sweden).

*Modupe, Prince, 1901– . *I Was a Savage*. New York: Harcourt, Brace, 1957, 185 pp. (French West Africa).

Morley, Helena (pseud.) see Brant, Alice (Dayrell).

*Mottram, Ralph Hale, 1883–1973. *Autobiography with a Difference*. New York: Appleton-Century, 1939, 287 pp. (England).

*——. *The Window Seat or Life Observed*. London: Hutchinson, 1954, 256 pp. (England).

*Muir, Edwin, 1887–1959. *The Story and the Fable: An Autobiography*. London: Harrap, 1940, 264 pp. (Scotland).

*Nabokov, Vladimir Vladimirovich, 1899–   . *Speak, Memory: A Memoir*. London: Gollancz, 1951, 237 pp. (Russia).

*Neilson, Elisabeth (Müser), 1882–   . *The House I Knew: Memories of Youth*. Boston: Houghton-Mifflin, 1941, 338 pp. (Germany).

Neumann, Robert. *Children of Vienna*. New York: Dutton, 1947, 223 pp. (Austria).

*Nexo, Martin Andersen, 1869–1954. *Under the Open Sky: My Early Years*. New York: Vanguard, 1938, 330 pp. (Denmark).

Nicolson, Harold George. *Helen's Tower*. New York: Harcourt, Brace, 1938, 297 pp. (England).

*Nielsen, Carl, 1865–1931. *My Childhood*. London: Hutchinson, 1953, 167 pp. (Denmark).

*Noyes, Pierrepont Burt, 1870–1959. *My Father's House: An Oneida Boyhood*. New York: Farrar and Rinehart, 1937, 312 pp. (U.S.A.).

*O'Casey, Sean, 1884–1964. *I Knock at the Door: Swift Glances Back

at Things That Made Me. New York: Macmillan, 1949, 294 pp. (Ire·
land).

*——. *Pictures in the Hallway.* New York: Macmillan, 1949, 373 pp.
(Ireland).

*O'Connor, Frank (Michael O'Donovan), 1903–1966. *An Only Child.*
New York: Knopf, 1961, 275 pp. (Ireland).

*Ogilvie, Mary I. *A Scottish Childhood and What Happened After.*
Oxford: George Ronald, 1952, 79 pp. (Scotland).

Olivier, Edith. *Love Child.* London: Richard, 1951, 158 pp. (England).

*O'Malley, Mary Dolling (Sanders), 1889–1939. *A Family of Two
Worlds: A Portrait of Her Mother.* New York: Macmillan, 1955, 244
pp. (U.S.A.).

*O'Sullivan, Maurice. *Twenty Years A-Growing.* London: Oxford,
1933, 298 pp. (Ireland).

*Pagnol, Marcel, 1895–   . *The Days Were Too Short.* Garden City,
New York: Doubleday, 1960, 335 pp. (France).

*Palmer, Herbert Edward. *The Mistletoe Child: An Autobiography of
Childhood.* London: Dent, 1935, 307 pp. (England).

*Paul, Leslie Allen, 1905– . *The Boy Down Kitchener Street.*
London: Faber and Faber, 1957, 191 pp. (England).

*——. *The Living Hedge.* London: Faber and Faber, 1946, 180 pp.
(England).

*Peck, Winifred. *Home for the Holidays.* London: Faber and Faber,
1955, 208 pp. (England).

*Phelps, Orra Almir (Parker), 1867–   . *When I Was a Girl in the
Martin Box.* New York: Island Press, 1949, 157 pp. (U.S.A.).

*Phillips, Margaret Mann, 1906– . *Within the City Wall: A Memoir
of Childhood.* Cambridge: Cambridge University Press, 1953, 123
pp. (U.S.A.).

*Pinchon, Edgcumb, 1883–   . *Until I Find: A Novel of Boyhood.*
New York: Knopf, 1936, 324 pp. (England).

*Plomer, William Charles Franklyn, 1903– . *Double Lives: An Auto-
biography.* London: Jonathan Cape, 1943, 216 pp. (South Africa).

*Posse, Amelie (Brázdová), 1884–   . *In the Beginning Was the
Light.* New York: Dutton, 1942, 410 pp. (Sweden).

*Potter, Stephen, 1900–1969. *Steps to Immaturity.* London: Hart-
Davis, 1959, 225 pp. (England).

Powell, Violet, 1912–   . *Five Out of Six: An Autobiography*. London: Heinemann, 1960, 248 pp. (England).

*Proust, Marcel, 1871–1922. *Swann's Way*. New York: Modern Library, 1928, 551 pp. (France).

Pryce-Jones, Alan (ed.). *Little Innocents: Childhood Reminiscences*. London: Cobden-Sanderson, 1932, 124 pp. (England).

*Quiller-Couch, Arthur Thomas, 1863–1944. *Memories and Opinions: An Unfinished Autobiography*. New York: Macmillan, 1945, 105 pp. (England).

*Ratel, Simonne, 1900–48. *The Green Grape*. New York: Macmillan, 1937, 307 pp. (France).

*——. *The House in the Hills*. New York: Macmillan, 1934, 291 pp. (France).

*Raverat, Gwendolen Mary (Darwin), 1885–1957. *Period Piece: A Cambridge Childhood*. London: Faber and Faber, 1952, 281 pp. (England).

Rawlings, Marjorie (Kinnan). *South Moon Under*. New York: Scribner's, 1933, 334 pp. (U.S.A.).

*Read, Herbert Edward, 1893–1968. *Annals of Innocence and Experience*. London: Faber and Faber, 1940, 211 pp. (England).

*——. *The Innocent Eye*. London: Faber and Faber, 1933, 81 pp. (England).

*Reid, Forrest, 1876–1947. *Apostate*. Boston: Houghton-Mifflin, 1926, 235 pp. (England).

——. *Peter Waring*. London: Faber and Faber, 1937, 374 pp. (England).

——. *The Retreat: or, The Machinations of Henry*. London: Faber and Faber, 1936, 299 pp. (England).

*Renan, Ernest, 1823–1892. *Recollections of My Youth*. London: Routledge, 1929, 380 pp. (France).

*Ripley, Thomas Emerson. *A Vermont Boyhood*. New York: Appleton-Century, 1937, 234 pp. (U.S.A.).

Roberts, Elizabeth Madox. *The Time of Man*. New York: Viking, 1926, 382 pp. (U.S.A.).

*Roberts, Jesse David, 1882–   . *Bears, Bibles and a Boy: Memories of the Adirondacks*. New York: Norton, 1961, 256 pp. (U.S.A.).

Robinson, Lennox. *Three Homes*. London: Joseph, 1938, 261 pp. (Ireland).

*Rodaway, Angela. *A London Childhood*. London: Batsford, 1960, 158 pp. (England).

*Ross Williamson, Hugh, 1901–   . *The Walled Garden: An Autobiography*. London: Joseph, 1956, 231 pp. (England).

*Rowse, A. L., 1903– . *A Cornish Childhood: Autobiography of a Cornishman*. London: Jonathan Cape, 1942, 282 pp. (England).

Ruark, Robert Chester. *The Old Man and the Boy*. New York: Holt, 1957, 303 pp. (U.S.A.).

*Rumbold, Richard. *My Father's Son*. London: Jonathan Cape, 1949, 223 pp. (England).

*Ruskin, John, 1819–1900. *Praeterita: Outlines of Scenes and Thoughts, Perhaps Worthy of Memory, in My Past Life*. Boston: Dana Estes, n.d., 459 pp. (England).

Sackville West, Edward. *Simpson: A Life*. London: Heinemann, 1931, 384 pp. (England).

*Saroyan, William, 1908– . *My Name is Aram*. New York: Harcourt, Brace, 1940, 220 pp. (U.S.A.).

*Sarton, May, 1912– . *I Knew a Phoenix: Sketches for an Autobiography*. New York: Rinehart, 1959, 222 pp. (Belgium; U.S.A.).

*Sassoon, Siegfried Lorraine, 1886–1967. *The Old Century and Seven More Years*. London: Faber and Faber, 1938, 293 pp. (England).

*Schweitzer, Albert, 1875–1965. *Memoirs of Childhood and Youth*. New York: Macmillan, 1925, 103 pp. (Germany).

Schwob, Marcel. *The Children's Crusade*. Portland, Maine: Thomas Mosher, 1905, 87 pp. (France).

*Sedgwick, Anne Douglas, 1873–1935. *A Childhood in Brittany: Eighty Years Ago*. Boston: Houghton-Mifflin, 1919, 224 pp. (France).

*Sender, Ramón José, 1901– . *Chronicle of Dawn*. Garden City, New York: Doubleday, 1944, 201 pp. (Spain).

*Sewell, Elizabeth, 1919– . *The Dividing of Time*. Garden City, New York: Doubleday, 1951, 249 pp. (England).

*Shepard, Ernest Howard, 1879–1974. *Drawn from Memory*. Philadelphia: Lippincott, 1957, 190 pp. (England).

*Shields, Karena. *The Changing Wind*. New York: Crowell, 1959, 215 pp. (Mexico).

**Singer, Dorothea (Waley). *Giordano Bruno: His Life and Thought*. New York: Schuman, 1950, 389 pp. (Italy).

Sitwell, Osbert Sacheverell, 1892–1969. *The Scarlet Tree*. Boston: Little, Brown, 1946, 381 pp. (England).

*——. *All Summer in a Day: An Autobiographical Fantasia*. London: Duckworth, 1931, 287 pp. (England).

*Skariatina, Irina. 1883–1962. *Little Era in Old Russia.* Indianapolis: Bobbs-Merrill, 1934, 392 pp. (Russia).

*Smith, Emma, 1923– . *A Cornish Waif's Story: An Autobiography.* New York: Dutton, 1956, 192 pp. (England).

*Smith, Robert Paul. *"Where Did You Go?" "Out." "What Did You Do?" "Nothing."* New York: Norton, 1957, 124 pp. (U.S.A.).

*Spring, Howard, 1889–1965. *Heaven Lies About Us: A Fragment of Infancy.* London: Constable, 1939, 106 pp. (Wales).

*Stafford, Jean, 1915– . *The Mountain Lion.* New York: Harcourt, Brace, 1947, 231 pp. (U.S.A.).

*Stark, Freya, 1926– . *Traveller's Prelude.* London: Murray, 1950, 346 pp. (England).

*Starkie, Enid, 1903–1971. *A Lady's Child.* London: Faber and Faber, 1941, 341 pp. (Ireland).

Still, James. *River of Earth.* New York: Viking, 1940, 245 pp. (U.S.A.).

Strong, Leonard Alfred George. *The Garden.* New York: Knopf, 1931, 351 pp. (Ireland).

*Sturt, George, 1863–1927. *A Small Boy in the Sixties.* Cambridge: Cambridge University Press, 1927, 240 pp. (England).

*Sullivan, Louis Henry, 1856–1924. *The Autobiography of an Idea.* New York: Dover, 1956, 329 pp. (U.S.A.).

*Symons, Dorothy Geraldine, 1909– . *Children in the Close.* London: Batsford, 1959, 183 pp. (England).

*Tallents, Stephen George, 1884–1958. *Man and Boy.* London: Faber and Faber, 1943, 431 pp. (England).

*Teale, Edwin Way, 1899– . *Dune Boy: The Early Years of a Naturalist.* New York: Dodd, Mead, 1943, 255 pp. (U.S.A.).

Tennant, Catherine Mary. *Peter the Wild Boy.* New York: Harper, 1939, 215 pp. (England).

*Thirkell, Angela, 1890–1961. *Three Houses.* London: Oxford University Press, 1931, 135 pp. (England).

*Thomas, Dylan, 1914–1953. *A Child's Christmas in Wales.* Norfolk, Connecticut: New Directions, 1954, 31 pp. (Wales).

*Thomas, Edward, 1878–1917. *The Childhood of Edward Thomas: A Fragment of Autobiography.* London: Faber and Faber, 1938, 152 pp. (England).

*Thompson, Ariadne. *The Octagonal Heart.* Indianapolis: Bobbs-Merrill, 1956, 221 pp. (U.S.A.).

*Thompson, Dorothy, 1894–1961. *Once on Christmas.* London: Oxford University Press, 1938, 43 pp. (U.S.A.).

*Thompson, Flora. *Lark Rise.* London: Oxford University Press, 1939, 288 pp. (England).

*——. *Over to Candleford.* London: Oxford University Press, 1941, 215 pp. (England).

*Tolstoy, Lev Nikolaevich, 1828–1910. *Childhood, Boyhood and Youth.* London: Oxford University Press, 1930, 404 pp. (Russia).

*Undset, Sigrid, 1882–1949. *The Longest Years.* New York: Knopf, 1935; 332 pp. (Norway).

*Uttley, Alison, 1884–   . *Ambush of Young Days.* London: Faber and Faber, 1937, 285 pp. (England).

——. *The Country Child.* London: Faber and Faber, 1931, 288 pp. (England).

*——. *Country Hoard.* London: Faber and Faber, 1943, 130 pp. (England).

*——. *The Farm on the Hill.* London: Faber and Faber, 1941, 316 pp. (England).

——. *High Meadows.* London: Faber and Faber, 1938, 371 pp. (England).

——. *A Traveler in Time.* London: Faber and Faber, 1939, 333 pp. (England).

*Van Druten, John, 1901–1957. *The Widening Circle.* London: Heinemann, 1957, 229 pp. (England).

Vaughan, Auriel Rosemary Malet. *My Bird Sings.* London: Faber and Faber, 1945, 185 pp. (France).

*Vaughan, Richard, 1904–1954. *There is a River.* New York: Dutton, 1961, 191 pp. (Wales).

*Verschoyle, Moira. *So Long to Wait: An Irish Childhood.* London: Bles, 1960, 181 pp. (Ireland).

*——. *Four to Fourteen by a Victorian Child.* London: Hale, 1939, 157 pp. (England).

**Wagenknecht, Edward Charles (ed.). *When I Was a Child: An Anthology.* New York: Dutton, 1946, 477 pp. (England; U.S.A.).

*Warren, Henry C. *A Boy in Kent.* London: Bles, 1937, 220 pp. (England).

*Welch, Denton. *A Voice Through a Cloud.* London: Readers Union, John Lehmann, 1951, 242 pp. (England).

*Whipple, Dorothy, 1893–   . *The Other Day: An Autobiography.* London: Joseph, 1936, 253 pp. (England).

*Wiener, Norbert, 1894–1964. *Ex-Prodigy: My Childhood and Youth.* New York: Simon and Schuster, 1953, 309 pp. (U.S.A.).

*Williams, Emlyn, 1905–   . *George: An Early Autobiography.* London: Hamish Hamilton, 1961, 461 pp. (Wales).

*Williamson, Henry, 1897–   . *The Children of Shallowford.* London: Faber and Faber, 1939, 292 pp. (England).

*Williamson, Richard Calvert. *The Dawn Is My Brother.* London: Faber and Faber, 1959, 191 pp. (England).

*Wingfield, Sheila, 1906–   . *Real People.* London: Cresset, 1952, 198 pp. (England).

*Woolf, Leonard Sidney, 1880–1969. *Sowing: An Autobiography of the Years 1880–1904.* New York: Harcourt, Brace, 1960, 224 pp. (England).

Woolf, Virginia (Stephen), 1882–1941. *The Waves.* London: L. and Virginia Woolf, 1931, 324 pp. (England).

*Wordsworth, William, 1770–1850. *The Prelude: or Growth of a Poet's Mind.* Oxford: Clarendon, 1926, 614 pp. (England).

*Wright, Richard, 1908–1960. *Black Boy: A Record of Childhood and Youth.* New York: Harper, 1945, 228 pp. (U.S.A.).

——. *The Long Dream: A Novel.* Garden City, New York: Doubleday, 1958, 384 pp. (U.S.A.).

*Yeats, William Butler, 1865–1939. *Autobiographies: Reveries Over Childhood and Youth; and The Trembling of the Veil.* New York: Macmillan, 1927, 447 pp. (Ireland).

*Young, Francis Brett, 1884–1954. *Wistanslow: An Unfinished Autobiographical Novel Based on Youthful Memories.* London: Heinemann, 1956, 157 pp. (England).

*Zhigalova, Olga. *Across the Green Past.* Chicago: Regnery, 1952, 214 pp. (Russia).

Index